Skills
for
Effective
Writing
3

CAMBRIDGE
UNIVERSITY PRESS

CAMBRIDGE
UNIVERSITY PRESS

32 Avenue of the Americas, New York, NY 10013-2473, USA

Cambridge University Press is part of the University of Cambridge.

It furthers the University's mission by disseminating knowledge in the pursuit of education, learning and research at the highest international levels of excellence.

www.cambridge.org
Information on this title: www.cambridge.org/9781107613560

© Cambridge University Press 2013

First published 2013
Reprinted 2015

Printed in Italy by Rotolito Lombarda S.p.A.

A catalogue record for this publication is available from the British Library

ISBN 978-1-107-61356-0 Student's Book

Cambridge University Press has no responsibility for the persistence or accuracy of URLs for external or third-party internet websites referred to in this publication, and does not guarantee that any content on such websites is, or will remain, accurate or appropriate.

The publisher wishes to acknowledge the contributions of the following writers:
Laurie Blass, Susan Hills, Hilary Hodge, Elizabeth Iannotti, Kathryn O'Dell, Lara Ravitch, and Eve Einselen Yu.

Art direction, book design, cover design, editorial management, layout services, and photo research: Hyphen S.A.

Cover image: ©Ingmar Bjork/Shutterstock.com

Photography: 2 ©iStockphoto/Thinkstock.com; 6 ©nmedia/Shutterstock.com; 10 ©Gina Smith/ Shutterstock.com; 14 ©Arvind Balaraman/Shutterstock.com; 18 ©Alexander Kirch/Shutterstock.com; 22 ©Zoonar/Thinkstock.com; 26 ©Stanislav Popov/Shutterstock.com; 30 ©Iv Mirin/Shutterstock.com; 34 ©iofoto/Shutterstock. com; 38 ©Sashkin/Shutterstock.com; 42 ©Yuri Arcurs/Shutterstock.com; 46 ©Golden Pixels LLC/Shutterstock.com; 50 ©iStockphoto/Thinkstock.com; 54 ©Jesse Kunerth/Shutterstock.com; 58 ©V. J. Matthew/Shutterstock.com; 62 ©iStockphoto/ Thinkstock.com; 66 ©Stephen Coburn/Shutterstock.com; 70 ©Jason Stitt/ Shutterstock.com; 74 ©Digital Vision/Thinkstock.com; 78 ©iStockphoto/Thinkstock. com; 82 ©anweber/Shutterstock.com; 86 ©Santiago Cornejo/Shutterstock.com; 90 ©Brand X Pictures/Thinkstock.com; 94 ©Toranico/Shutterstock.com; 98 ©iStockphoto/Shutterstock.com; 102 ©Inga Nielsen/Shutterstock.com; 106 ©Morgan Lane Photography/Shutterstock.com; 110 ©Ingram Publishing/Thinkstock.com

Skills for Effective Writing 3

CAMBRIDGE
UNIVERSITY PRESS

Contents

Discrete writing skills, such as creating topic sentences and recognizing irrelevant information, are critical for good writers. This 4-level series teaches these skills and offers extensive practice opportunities.

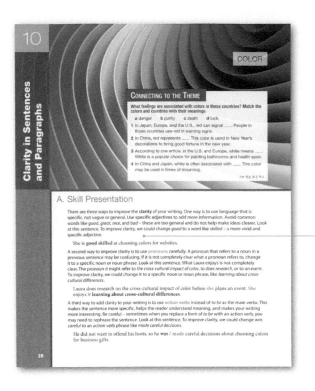

SKILL PRESENTATION

Each unit teaches a single discrete writing skill, helping students focus their attention on developing the skill fully.

OVER TO YOU

Following instruction, students are eased into the skill's application, facilitating their understanding of exactly how each skill works.

When students master these skills, all of their writing improves. This allows teachers to focus their time and feedback on the content of student work.

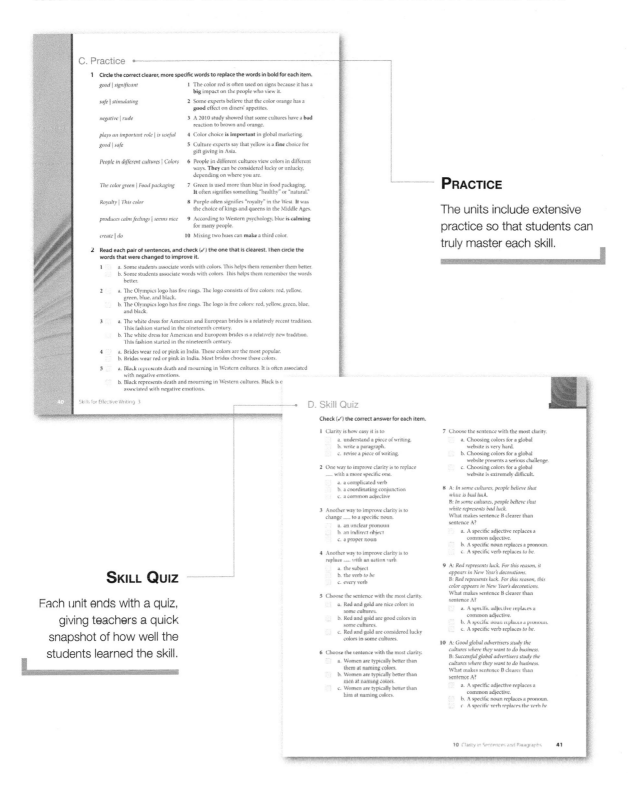

PRACTICE

The units include extensive practice so that students can truly master each skill.

SKILL QUIZ

Each unit ends with a quiz, giving teachers a quick snapshot of how well the students learned the skill.

Simple, Compound, and Complex Sentences

FIRST IMPRESSIONS

CONNECTING TO THE THEME

What can you do to make a good first impression? Which of the tips below do you think may help?

1 You should be neat and well-dressed.

2 You should make eye contact with the other person.

3 You should talk a lot about yourself.

4 You should be comfortable, but you shouldn't look too casual.

5 You should ask about the other person when the time is right.

1, 2, 4, and 5 will help you make a good first impression.

A. Skill Presentation

When you write, you should use a combination of simple, compound, and complex sentences.

A **simple sentence** has one or more subjects and one or more verbs. It has only one **independent clause** and expresses only one complete idea. Both of the following simple sentences have one independent clause, but the number of subjects and verbs varies.

Ethan is confident. (1 subject + 1 verb)

Ethan and Vicky feel important and look confident. (2 subjects + 2 verbs)

A **compound sentence** has two or more subjects and two or more verbs. It has at least two related independent clauses that are joined by a **coordinating conjunction**, such as *and*, *but*, *or*, or *so*.

— INDEPENDENT CLAUSE — ——— INDEPENDENT CLAUSE ———
Ethan is confident, **and** he makes a good first impression.

Ethan and Vicky are confident, **but** their sister isn't confident at all.

A **complex sentence** has two or more subjects and two or more verbs. It has an independent clause that is connected to a **dependent clause**. The dependent clause starts with a **subordinating conjunction**, such as *after*, *before*, *when*, *because*, *although*, or *if*.

— INDEPENDENT CLAUSE — ——————— DEPENDENT CLAUSE ———————
Ethan is usually selfish, **although** he sometimes thinks of other people.

Ethan will get the job **if** he makes a good impression.

B. Over to You

1 **Read the sentences. Decide if they are simple, compound, or complex. Write *S* for Simple, *C* for Compound, or *CX* for Complex.**

___ **1** Tom made a good impression, so he got the job.

___ **2** Jason seems friendly, although he is very shy.

___ **3** Nancy and Lorena have a lot of friends.

2 **Read the paragraph and check (✓) the correct answers.**

> **First impressions are important in an interview.** *You will make a good impression if you follow some important steps.* **Confident people often make good first impressions.** *Employers may feel uncomfortable when you do not seem confident.* **Your clothing can also make a good first impression.** <u>Clean and neat clothing makes a good impression, and a neat hairstyle also shows professionalism.</u> *Messy clothing does not make a good impression because people associate it with laziness.* <u>You do not have to wear expensive clothing, but you can still dress nicely.</u> **Finally, your body language says a lot about you.** *You should not move around too much, although you do not have to be perfectly still.* **You can follow this advice for your next interview.**

1 The sentences in **bold** are

☐ a. simple sentences.
☐ b. compound sentences.
☐ c. complex sentences.

2 The *italicized* sentences are

☐ a. simple sentences.
☐ b. compound sentences.
☐ c. complex sentences.

3 The <u>underlined</u> sentences are

☐ a. simple sentences.
☐ b. compound sentences.
☐ c. complex sentences.

CHECK!

1 A _____ sentence has at least one subject and at least one _____. It has only one independent clause.

2 A _____ sentence has at least two subjects and at least two verbs. It has at least two _____ clauses that are related to each other.

2 A _____ sentence has at least two subjects and at least two verbs. It has a _____ clause that is connected to an independent clause.

C. Practice

1 **Read each sentence in the chart. Decide if it is simple, compound, or complex. Check (✓) the box in the correct column.**

	SIMPLE SENTENCE	COMPOUND SENTENCE	COMPLEX SENTENCE
1. Confident people are usually happy.			
2. Cheerful people often get jobs easily because they are usually pleasant coworkers.			
3. My friend Jenny makes a bad first impression.			
4. Jenny seems negative when she meets people for the first time.			
5. She has friends, but she does not always keep them for very long.			
6. Negative people usually do not get jobs easily, but Jenny found a good job.			
7. Negative people can be unreasonable, and they can be difficult to work with.			
8. Negative people have many unpleasant characteristics, although they have good ones, too.			
9. Jenny likes telling jokes and making people laugh.			
10. Jenny is a good worker because she has many positive characteristics.			

2 **Read the sentences. Write the number of independent and dependent clauses. If there are no clauses of a certain type, write X.**

1 The new employee made a positive first impression.
___ independent clause(s), ___ dependent clause(s)

2 Employers often look at your clothing, so you should dress nicely for an interview.
___ independent clause(s), ___ dependent clause(s)

3 John had a good interview, although his dirty suit made a bad first impression.
___ independent clause(s), ___ dependent clause(s)

4 Mario is a great leader because he is passionate about his work.
___ independent clause(s), ___ dependent clause(s)

5 Kim and Jocelyn are not very good leaders.
___ independent clause(s), ___ dependent clause(s)

6 Some people make judgments about others, but first impressions are not always correct.
___ independent clause(s), ___ dependent clause(s)

7 Employers sometimes make incorrect judgments about workers.
___ independent clause(s), ___ dependent clause(s)

D. Skill Quiz

Check (✓) the correct answer for each item.

1 Which phrase describes a simple sentence?
   - [ ] a. two or more subjects, two or more verbs, two independent clauses
   - [ ] b. two or more subjects, two or more verbs, an independent clause, a dependent clause
   - [ ] c. one or more subjects, one or more verbs, one independent clause

2 Which phrase describes a compound sentence?
   - [ ] a. two or more subjects, two or more verbs, two independent clauses
   - [ ] b. two or more subjects, two or more verbs, an independent clause, a dependent clause
   - [ ] c. one or more subjects, one or more verbs, one independent clause

3 Which phrase describes a complex sentence?
   - [ ] a. two or more subjects, two or more verbs, two independent clauses
   - [ ] b. two or more subjects, two or more verbs, one independent clause, one dependent clause
   - [ ] c. one or more subjects, one or more verbs, one independent clause

4 When you write a paragraph, you can include
   - [ ] a. only simple sentences.
   - [ ] b. simple, compound, and complex sentences.
   - [ ] c. exactly one compound sentence and one complex sentence.

5 *Good employees arrive on time.*
   How many dependent clauses does this sentence have?
   - [ ] a. zero
   - [ ] b. one
   - [ ] c. two

6 *Managers need to listen to people if there is a problem.*
   How many independent clauses does this sentence have?
   - [ ] a. zero
   - [ ] b. one
   - [ ] c. two

7 *Employers should not hire people based on personal judgments, and they should not pay attention to stereotypes.*
   How many independent clauses does this sentence have?
   - [ ] a. one
   - [ ] b. two
   - [ ] c. three

8 *Joanna and Kyle form opinions about others quickly.*
   What type of sentence is this?
   - [ ] a. simple
   - [ ] b. compound
   - [ ] c. complex

9 *Opinions may be incorrect if they are based on personal preferences.*
   What type of sentence is this?
   - [ ] a. simple
   - [ ] b. compound
   - [ ] c. complex

10 *Mark did not make a good impression, so Mr. Weston did not hire him.*
   What type of sentence is this?
   - [ ] a. simple
   - [ ] b. compound
   - [ ] c. complex

GLOBAL MARKETING

CONNECTING TO THE THEME

The Internet is the most important tool in global marketing today. Which of these are reasons why?

1 Word-of-mouth advertising, or hearing about products from people you know, does not impact as many people as the Internet does.

2 Social networking sites are popular.

3 More than 75 percent of social media users have bought something because of an ad or comment they saw online.

4 Some businesses do not have an Internet presence.

1 and 3 are two reasons why the Internet plays an important role in global marketing.

A. Skill Presentation

A **paragraph** usually starts with a **topic sentence**. The topic sentence states the main idea of the paragraph. There are also supporting sentences. They give more information, such as details, examples, or facts, to support the main idea. A paragraph also has a concluding sentence. This can summarize the ideas in the paragraph or restate the main idea.

A good paragraph has ideas that relate to each other. All sentences should relate to the main idea in the topic sentence. Supporting sentences that relate to the main idea are relevant. If a sentence is not related, it is irrelevant. Avoid irrelevant sentences when you write.

Read the beginning of this paragraph. Think about the features of a good paragraph as you read.

> ^TS^People use a variety of interactive websites. ^SS^**For example**, people use social networking sites to share information. ^SS^People also use them to keep in touch with friends. ^SS^~~Most people who work for social networking sites enjoy their jobs.~~ ^SS^**In addition**, Internet phone and messaging services are also popular. ^CS^There are many kinds of interactive websites in use today, for many different reasons.

The third supporting sentence is not related to the main idea. It is irrelevant, and it should not be included in this paragraph.

Supporting sentences should also be organized logically and should be connected. Use **transition words** and **phrases** to do this. Transition words such as *first*, *second*, and *then* and transition phrases like *for example*, *another example*, and *in addition* can help readers follow your ideas more easily. Look at the paragraph above again. The transition phrases *for example* and *in addition* help organize the supporting sentences logically.

B. Over to You

1 Read the paragraph and circle the correct answers for each item.

¹At MuchMarket, we use interactive websites to help sell products. ²For example, we use customer reviews to get new customers. ³In addition, we use social networking sites to communicate with customers. ⁴We pay our employees a lot and give them paid vacations. ⁵We love to use the newest technology to attract new customers.

1 Which sentence does not relate to the main idea?

Sentence 2 | Sentence 3 | Sentence 4

2 Which transition phrases connect supporting sentences?

At MuchMarket, | we use | For example, | In addition, | help sell products, | with customers

2 Read the topic sentence. Decide if the sentences support or provide a conclusion for the topic sentence. Write *Y* for Yes or *N* for No.

Topic Sentence: These days, businesses are trying to spend less money on advertising.

____ **1** For example, some companies are not giving employees pay raises, and they are not offering extra vacation time.

____ **2** Other companies are using free online tools to advertise their products.

____ **3** Some websites offer high-quality products that are still affordable.

____ **4** Companies are finding many ways to lower their advertising costs today.

____ **5** Spending money on advertising can increase profits.

____ **6** Companies that can save money on advertising can use the cash elsewhere.

____ **7** More and more effort is being made by businesses to cut the amount of money they spend on advertising.

____ **8** Social networking sites can be a great way to generate interest in a product without spending any money at all.

CHECK!

1 A *good* | *bad* paragraph has a topic sentence, supporting sentences, and a concluding sentence.

2 A good paragraph includes only *relevant* | *irrelevant* supporting sentences, not *relevant* | *irrelevant* supporting sentences.

3 A good paragraph also has sentences that are organized *transitionally* | *logically* and uses *logic* | *transition* words and phrases correctly.

C. Practice

1   Read the paragraph. Underline three sentences that are irrelevant.

¹Video-sharing websites can help businesses. ²First, many companies can save money by advertising on these sites. ³A local business, for example, can make a video and post it for free. ⁴Famous actors sometimes earn a lot of money. ⁵Next, businesses can often find new customers by sharing videos online. ⁶For example, an American company may be able to reach a more global market. ⁷Many Americans think other cultures are truly interesting. ⁸Finally, friends can use video-sharing sites to share videos of special events, such as graduation. ⁹There are many ways that businesses can use video-sharing websites to sell their products.

2   Read the paragraph and circle the correct transition words to help connect the ideas.

The restaurant Mimi had a great year. The owner decided to use free online tools to reach more customers. *First,* | *Then,* | *After that*, he created an account on a popular social networking site. *Then,* | *First,* | *In conclusion*, he posted information about the restaurant, including its location, the menu, and a list of daily specials. *After that,* | *In conclusion,* | *Finally*, he took pictures of happy customers and posted them on the site. *Finally,* | *To start,* | *Second*, he asked frequent customers to write reviews on the site. Soon the site was very busy, and the restaurant was full.

3   Read the paragraph and answer the questions.

> ### Virtual Word-of-Mouth Marketing
>
> ¹Innovative businesses are now using virtual, or online, word-of-mouth advertising. ²Have you ever bought something because a friend said, "I love it!"? ³Most people have. ⁴In fact, a 2009 study found that 90 percent of people trust word-of-mouth advertising more than any other kind. ⁵Review websites allow customers to write their opinions about businesses. ⁶Other people then read the reviews before making decisions about what to buy. ⁷Some businesses also use social networking sites to post frequent updates. ⁸People read these updates and tell their friends about them. ⁹For example, Kogi, a mobile food truck in Los Angeles, gives information about its location several times a day. ¹⁰Over 50,000 fans follow these updates. ¹¹They buy food when a Kogi truck is nearby. ¹²In addition, they often tell their friends. ¹³Clever businesses are finding new ways to use websites to promote their products more effectively.

1 Which sentence is the topic sentence? ___

2 Which sentence gives a fact about how many people trust word-of-mouth advertising?

3 Which sentences describe how people use review websites? _____

4 Which sentences describe how businesses use social networking sites? _____

5 Which transition words are used to connect ideas? _____

6 Which sentence summarizes the main idea? _____

D. Skill Quiz

Check (✓) the correct answer for each item.

1 The ___ sentence expresses the main idea of a paragraph.
   - ☐ a. topic
   - ☐ b. supporting
   - ☐ c. concluding

2 ___ sentences give more information about the topic sentence.
   - ☐ a. Independent
   - ☐ b. Supporting
   - ☐ c. Factual

3 A good paragraph has
   - ☐ a. only sentences related to the main idea.
   - ☐ b. one or more irrelevant sentences.
   - ☐ c. only one relevant sentence.

4 Use transition words to
   - ☐ a. make an idea relevant.
   - ☐ b. format your paragraph correctly.
   - ☐ c. help organize supporting sentences.

5 Choose the most appropriate transition phrase for this paragraph:
   Review websites help companies sell products. ___, online reviews are helpful for getting new customers. Social networking sites are also useful.
   - ☐ a. In addition
   - ☐ b. For example
   - ☐ c. After that

6 Choose a relevant supporting sentence for this topic sentence: *Many people read customer reviews when they shop online.*
   - ☐ a. Customers use credit or debit cards to pay for things online.
   - ☐ b. Online advertisements may be inappropriate for different cultures.
   - ☐ c. In fact, more than 60 percent of shoppers read others' comments before deciding which product to buy.

7 Choose the irrelevant sentence in this paragraph:
   Some businesses post frequent updates on websites. People read these updates and tell friends. The best businesses treat their customers well. Clever businesses use these sites to sell products.
   - ☐ a. The best businesses treat their customers well.
   - ☐ b. Clever businesses use these sites to sell products.
   - ☐ c. People read these updates and tell friends.

8 Choose a relevant supporting sentence for this topic sentence: *There are many examples of word-of-mouth advertising online.*
   - ☐ a. You can see posters for new products in many cities.
   - ☐ b. You can find businesses advertising on video-sharing websites.
   - ☐ c. You can make many friends on social networking sites.

9 Choose a relevant concluding sentence to match this topic sentence: *Word-of-mouth advertising can be anything from talking to a friend to watching videos online.*
   - ☐ a. Teens spend more time sending messages than talking on the phone.
   - ☐ b. In everyday life, there are many types of word-of-mouth advertising.
   - ☐ c. Word-of-mouth advertising is a good way to make new friends.

10 Choose the transition words to help organize the sentences in this paragraph:
   It is easy to sign up on a video-sharing website. ___, you click on "Sign up." ___, you create a user name.
   - ☐ a. First, Then
   - ☐ b. After that, Finally
   - ☐ c. For example, In addition

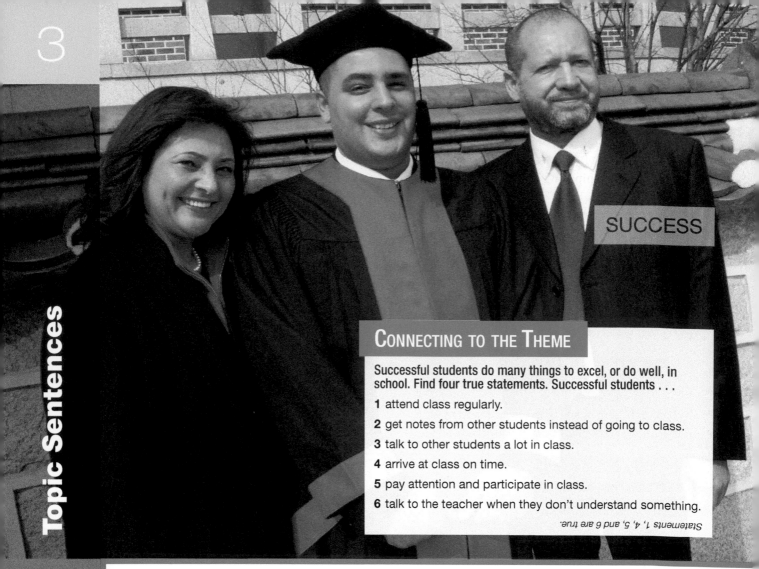

SUCCESS

CONNECTING TO THE THEME

Successful students do many things to excel, or do well, in school. Find four true statements. Successful students . . .

1 attend class regularly.

2 get notes from other students instead of going to class.

3 talk to other students a lot in class.

4 arrive at class on time.

5 pay attention and participate in class.

6 talk to the teacher when they don't understand something.

Statements 1, 4, 5, and 6 are true.

Topic Sentences

A. Skill Presentation

The **topic sentence** tells the main idea of a paragraph. Other sentences in the paragraph relate to this main idea. It is usually the first sentence in the paragraph, but not always. A topic sentence has two parts, the **topic** and the controlling idea. The topic tells the reader who or what the paragraph is about. It is usually a noun. The controlling idea tells what kind of information you will give about the topic in your paragraph. Look at this topic sentence.

——— **TOPIC** ——— ——— CONTROLLING IDEA ———
Successful students do many things to excel in school.

The topic is *successful students*. This tells the reader the paragraph will be about successful students. The controlling idea is *do many things to excel in school*. This focuses the topic and tells the reader that the paragraph will give information about things successful students do to excel in school. Now look at another topic sentence.

——— **TOPIC** ——— —— CONTROLLING IDEA ——
Successful students often make great leaders.

The topic of this sentence is also *successful students*, but the controlling idea is *often make great leaders*. This focuses the topic and tells the reader that the paragraph will give information about successful students being great leaders.

B. Over to You

1 **Read the topic sentences. Decide what are the topics and what are the controlling ideas. Circle the topics. Underline the controlling ideas.**

1 Students who are successful leaders inspire other people.

2 Scholarships give many students a chance to attend college.

3 Political leaders often inspire people to change society.

4 Success at college can lead to many different opportunities to make a difference.

2 **Read the paragraphs and choose the correct topic sentence for each one. There are two extra sentences.**

1 ___ They set an example for other students. Other students tend to listen to their ideas. Many successful students inspire others to do well. Students who are struggling may even depend on successful students for help. Students who are successful often have important positions, like class president. They usually make good leaders.

2 Who is Leymah Gbowee? ___ Gbowee has been fighting for peace for more than a decade. She has completed many programs that teach skills for peace building. She started an organization called Women Peace and Security Network Africa. She has won awards for her peace-building skills. She contributes her knowledge and helps guide the peace process. Gbowee promotes peace through her leadership.

a Many successful businessmen did well in school.
b Leymah Gbowee was born in Liberia in Africa.
c Successful students are often good leaders.
d Leymah Gbowee is a leader who promotes peace.

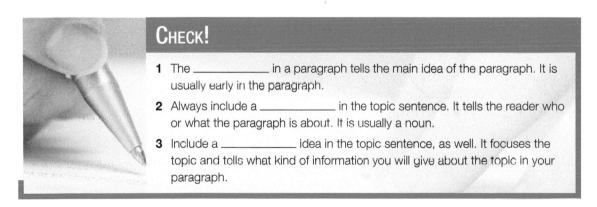

CHECK!

1 The _____ in a paragraph tells the main idea of the paragraph. It is usually early in the paragraph.

2 Always include a _____ in the topic sentence. It tells the reader who or what the paragraph is about. It is usually a noun.

3 Include a _____ idea in the topic sentence, as well. It focuses the topic and tells what kind of information you will give about the topic in your paragraph.

C. Practice

1 Read each topic sentence in the chart. Decide if the part in bold is the topic or the controlling idea. Check (✓) the box in the correct column.

	TOPIC	CONTROLLING IDEA
1. **Scholarships** are a good way to help pay for school.		
2. Scholarships **are a good way to help pay for school.**		
3. Mahatma Gandhi **promoted peace and nonviolence.**		
4. **Mahatma Gandhi** promoted peace and nonviolence.		
5. **Peaceful leaders** often achieve success.		
6. Peaceful leaders **often achieve success.**		
7. **The definition of "independent"** varies across time and cultures.		
8. The definition of "independent" **varies across time and cultures.**		
9. The Carter Center **contributes to world peace in various ways.**		
10. **The Carter Center** contributes to world peace in various ways.		

2 Read each topic sentence and circle the correct answer for each item.

1 Some leaders promote peace in their countries.
The topic is *peace | some leaders | their countries.*

2 The definition of "respect" varies across time.
The controlling idea is that the definition of "respect" *is different at different times | is always the same | is in the dictionary.*

3 Successful leaders are respected around the world.
The topic is *the world | respect | successful leaders.*

4 Peaceful movements can change the world.
The controlling idea is that peaceful movements *can make the world different | are always effective | may exist.*

5 Many wealthy people contribute money to help improve bad situations.
The topic is *money | many wealthy people | bad situations.*

6 Bill Gates achieved great wealth as the head of Microsoft.
This paragraph will give information about how Bill Gates *became wealthy | stayed busy | retired from Microsoft.*

7 The Bill and Melinda Gates Foundation has helped many people around the world.
The topic is *people around the world | Bill Gates | the Bill and Melinda Gates Foundation.*

8 Some college programs promote independent thinking.
This paragraph will give information about how some college programs *encourage people to think independently | want everyone to think the same way | offer only a few majors.*

D. Skill Quiz

Check (✓) the correct answer for each item.

1 What does the topic sentence of a paragraph do?
- ☐ a. gives information about several different topics
- ☐ b. tells the main idea of the paragraph
- ☐ c. gives examples of the topic

2 The topic sentence of a paragraph is usually
- ☐ a. the first or second sentence.
- ☐ b. in the middle of the paragraph.
- ☐ c. the last sentence.

3 What does the topic of a topic sentence tell the reader?
- ☐ a. what the title of the paragraph is
- ☐ b. who or what the paragraph is about
- ☐ c. the specific information the paragraph will give

4 What does the controlling idea of a topic sentence tell the reader?
- ☐ a. what the title of the paragraph is
- ☐ b. what the main subject of the paragraph is
- ☐ c. the information the paragraph will give about the topic

5 *Study groups help students succeed in college.*
What is the topic in this topic sentence?
- ☐ a. study groups
- ☐ b. college students
- ☐ c. success in college

6 *Grants can help pay for a student's education.*
What is the topic in this topic sentence?
- ☐ a. a student
- ☐ b. grants
- ☐ c. education

7 *Bill and Melinda Gates founded an organization to help people around the world.*
What is the topic in this topic sentence?
- ☐ a. people around the world
- ☐ b. an organization
- ☐ c. Bill and Melinda Gates

8 *Mahatma Gandhi succeeded by inspiring many people.*
What is the controlling idea in this topic sentence?
- ☐ a. why inspiring many people made Gandhi successful
- ☐ b. why people inspired Gandhi to be successful
- ☐ c. why different people define success in different ways

9 *The Carter Center works to bring peace to the world.*
What is the controlling idea in this topic sentence?
- ☐ a. how peace organizations are usually effective
- ☐ b. how The Carter Center tries to make the world more peaceful
- ☐ c. how The Carter Center guides world leaders

10 *Political leaders often inspire people around the world.*
What is the controlling idea in this topic sentence?
- ☐ a. ways that people everywhere are inspired by political leaders
- ☐ b. ways that inspirational people vote for good leaders
- ☐ c. ways that leaders inspire people to travel

NATURE VS. NURTURE

Supporting Sentences

A. Skill Presentation

A paragraph is a group of sentences about one topic. It starts with a **topic sentence**, which tells the main idea of a paragraph. The sentences that support the topic sentence are called supporting sentences. Supporting sentences are related to the topic sentence, and they are specific. They often answer the questions *who, what, when, where, why,* and *how* by giving facts, examples, or other details. Look at this example. This supporting sentence answers the question *What is meant by nature?*

> TSOne study suggests that intelligence is determined by nature. SS*Nature* means the characteristics a person gets from their parents.

Now let's add a second supporting sentence. This supporting sentence adds details that answer the question *What happened in the study?*

> SSSeveral twins, who share many characteristics, took an intelligence test and got similar scores.

It is important to make sure that all the supporting sentences in your paragraph are closely related to the topic sentence. Irrelevant sentences are sentences that are not related to the topic sentence. They can make your writing confusing and difficult to follow.

B. Over to You

1   **Read the topic sentence. Decide if each supporting sentence in the chart is related or unrelated. Check (✓) the box in the correct column.**

Topic Sentence: The Minnesota Center for Twin and Family Research is currently doing an interesting study about twins.

	RELATED (RELEVANT)	UNRELATED (IRRELEVANT)
1. It examines how nature and nurture affect twins.		
2. Researchers at the center hope to learn more about human development from this study.		
3. More than 5,000 people have participated in the study.		
4. Some twins do not look alike.		

2   **Read the sentences from a paragraph about Gregor Mendel. Check (✓) the two sentences that are unrelated to the topic sentence.**

Topic Sentence: Gregor Mendel was an important researcher.

☐   a. His research helped people learn about how nature affects living things.
☐   b. Mendel did several studies during the nineteenth century.
☐   c. He looked at similarities between related pea plants.
☐   d. Friedrich Franz was Mendel's teacher at the University of Olomouc.
☐   e. Mendel's experiments with pea plants were some of the first studies about genetics, or the study of genes.
☐   f. After doing these studies, Mendel said that some genes are stronger than others.
☐   g. Lucien Cuénot was also a leader in the field of genetics.
☐   h. Many of Mendel's ideas are still used today.

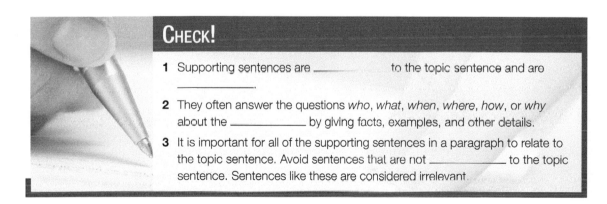

CHECK!

1   Supporting sentences are _____ to the topic sentence and are _____.

2   They often answer the questions *who*, *what*, *when*, *where*, *how*, or *why* about the _____ by giving facts, examples, and other details.

3   It is important for all of the supporting sentences in a paragraph to relate to the topic sentence. Avoid sentences that are not _____ to the topic sentence. Sentences like these are considered irrelevant.

C. Practice

1 **Read each supporting sentence in the chart. Decide which topic sentence it is related to. Check (✓) the box in the correct column.**

Topic Sentence 1: Genetics is an important scientific field.

Topic Sentence 2: Dominant genes are more powerful than others.

	TOPIC SENTENCE 1	TOPIC SENTENCE 2
1. Genetics is the study of how characteristics are passed through genes.		
2. For example, the gene for brown eyes is stronger than the gene for blue eyes.		
3. Scientists who study genetics have learned a lot about human behavior.		
4. Genes help determine many physical characteristics.		
5. Scientists who study genetics are called geneticists.		
6. Genes that are less strong are called recessive genes.		
7. It can help explain which traits people get from their parents.		
8. One reason more people have dark hair than light hair is because the gene for dark hair is stronger.		
9. Geneticists want to understand why family members often have similar diseases.		

2 **Read the two topic sentences in the chart. For each one, choose three supporting sentences that answer the questions who, where, and when. Write the letters of the correct supporting sentences in the boxes in the correct columns.**

	WHO?	WHERE?	WHEN?
1. Many geneticists did studies similar to the ones Mendel started.			
2. Howard Gardner believes people have several different kinds of intelligence.			

a Cuénot did his studies during the twentieth century.

b He does research at Harvard University.

c Lucien Cuénot did genetic research on plants and animals.

d In 1983, he published a book about multiple intelligences.

e He was the first person to describe multiple intelligences.

f Cuénot also worked in Europe.

D. Skill Quiz

Check (✓) the correct answer for each item.

1 Supporting sentences are
- ☐ a. related to the topic sentence.
- ☐ b. unrelated to the topic sentence.
- ☐ c. general and not specific.

2 Supporting sentences often
- ☐ a. list all questions related to the main idea.
- ☐ b. ask a question.
- ☐ c. answer a question like *Why?*

3 Supporting sentences that are unrelated to the topic sentence can make your writing
- ☐ a. stronger.
- ☐ b. more confusing.
- ☐ c. easier to read.

4 Choose the best supporting sentence for this topic sentence: *Twins that are separated at birth have many similarities.*
- ☐ a. The differences are also interesting, such as liking different foods.
- ☐ b. Many cousins are also similar.
- ☐ c. Studies show twins raised apart score similarly on intelligence tests.

5 Choose the best supporting sentence for this topic sentence: *According to Howard Gardner, there are many kinds of intelligences.*
- ☐ a. Some scientists use intelligence tests in their studies.
- ☐ b. "Emotional intelligence" means how well you understand emotions.
- ☐ c. The Michigan Research Center tested twins' intelligence.

6 Choose the supporting sentence that is unrelated to this topic sentence: *Many researchers study DNA.*
- ☐ a. DNA carries genetic information.
- ☐ b. Scientists are fascinated by twins.
- ☐ c. One organization in the U.S. has over 50 genetic researchers.

7 Choose the supporting sentence that is unrelated to this topic sentence: *Cuénot and Mendel were important geneticists.*
- ☐ a. Scientists agree that Cuénot's and Mendel's studies were significant.
- ☐ b. They helped us understand more about the role of nature.
- ☐ c. Other scientists believe that people have emotional intelligence.

8 Choose the supporting sentence that answers the question *Who has the same DNA?* for this topic sentence: *People with identical genes have identical DNA.*
- ☐ a. DNA is located inside the cells of all living things.
- ☐ b. Therefore, identical twins have matching DNA.
- ☐ c. It is an important part of biology.

9 Choose the supporting sentence that answers the question *What is eyesight?* for this topic sentence: *Poor eyesight is partly the result of genetics.*
- ☐ a. Eyesight is how well a person sees.
- ☐ b. Children who have two parents with poor vision will be affected.
- ☐ c. This is because genes contain some information about vision.

10 Choose the supporting sentence that answers the question *Who was Gregor Mendel?* for this topic sentence: *Modern genetics was founded by Gregor Mendel.*
- ☐ a. Research was done in several European countries.
- ☐ b. It was founded during the middle of the nineteenth century.
- ☐ c. Gregor Mendel was an Austrian scientist.

Concluding Sentences

LOOKING AHEAD AT TECHNOLOGY

CONNECTING TO THE THEME

Which of these products do you think will be available in the next ten years?

Several new and exciting products are expected to come onto the market in the next ten years. One manufacturer is creating voice-controlled TVs. Another is researching chips that could be implanted in the brain to allow you to "think" directions to a computer. One product that is close to becoming real is a system that automatically controls the lights, heat, and other things in the home. It's a very exciting time for technology and for the people who use it.

Any of these products could be widely available.

A. Skill Presentation

Most paragraphs end with a **concluding sentence**. It is usually the last sentence of the paragraph. You can write a concluding sentence in several ways. You can

1 **restate the main idea** from the topic sentence using different words.
2 offer a suggestion about the topic.
3 make a prediction about the topic.

It is important to remember that a good concluding sentence does not introduce a new idea.

Look at this topic sentence for a paragraph about 3D TVs and three different possible concluding sentences for the same paragraph.

3D TV is a relatively new technology that is becoming more popular.

[1]To conclude, the popularity of 3D TV is increasing.
[2]For these reasons, you may wish to wait to buy a 3D TV.
[3]In conclusion, most people will probably have 3D TVs in the future.

The first concluding sentence restates the main idea that 3D TV is relatively new and that it is becoming more popular. The second concluding sentence offers readers a suggestion – that they wait to buy a 3D TV. The third concluding sentence makes a prediction – that in the future, most people will own 3D TVs.

B. Over to You

1 Read the topic sentence and four concluding sentences. Three are correct for the paragraph. One is not correct because it introduces a new idea. Check (✓) the three appropriate concluding sentences.

Topic Sentence: Seoul is a world leader in technology.

☐ a. In summary, many new technologies are developed in Seoul.
☐ b. For this reason, you should visit Seoul to get the most modern products.
☐ c. To conclude, Seoul has wonderful food in their night markets.
☐ d. In conclusion, technology companies in Seoul will probably succeed in the years ahead.

2 Match each topic sentence (1–7) with the correct concluding sentence (a–g).

___ **1** 3D TVs are now available in many places.

___ **2** 3D TVs will likely be cheaper in the future.

___ **3** Internet service in Taipei is fairly cheap, usually costing about $13 a month.

___ **4** Taipei is known for its excellent, fast, wireless Internet.

___ **5** The city of Taipei started an online course in Internet skills.

___ **6** The prices of many popular gadgets are decreasing.

___ **7** Smartphones often have high-quality cameras.

a In conclusion, people in Taipei should take advantage of the training course to improve their Internet skills.

b For these reasons, some people buy smartphones with cameras instead of separate digital cameras.

c For this reason, it is probably best to wait a few years to buy a 3D TV.

d In conclusion, Taipei's wireless Internet service will probably continue to improve in the future.

e For this reason, some people suggest waiting to buy a new phone or e-reader.

f To conclude, it is possible to buy a 3D TV in many electronics stores.

g In summary, Internet service in Taipei is not very expensive.

CHECK!

1 A concluding sentence is usually the *first* | *last* sentence of the paragraph.

2 It can *state* | *restate* the main idea from the topic sentence, offer *a suggestion* | *new information* about the topic, or *make a prediction* | *tell the history* about the topic.

3 A concluding sentence *does not* | *does* introduce a new idea.

C. Practice

1 Read the topic sentences. Decide if the sentences that follow are good concluding sentences or not. Write *G* for Good or *NG* for Not Good.

1 Handheld devices are getting smaller every year.

_____ a. To conclude, it may make sense to wait a year or two to buy a smaller gadget.

_____ b. To conclude, some 3D TVs are small, but most are large.

_____ c. In summary, the size of handheld devices decreases each year.

_____ d. In summary, larger handheld devices are often less expensive.

2 Many people depend on the Internet to get news.

_____ a. In summary, newspapers and magazines are not very expensive.

_____ b. In summary, many people read news online.

_____ c. In conclusion, the cost of Internet services will probably decrease in the future.

_____ d. In conclusion, even more people will probably get their news online in the future.

3 3D technology for TVs is improving rapidly.

_____ a. To summarize, improvements are quickly being made to 3D televisions.

_____ b. For these reasons, 3D TV will be even better in a few years.

_____ c. For these reasons, interactive TV shows may become more popular.

_____ d. To summarize, flat screen TVs are cheaper than they were a few years ago.

2 Read the paragraph and check (✓) three sentences that would make good concluding sentences.

Stockholm, Sweden, is a city where it is easy to connect to the Internet. The connection is usually very fast, although it can be expensive. Stockholm has a number of Internet cafés that are essential for many people. People go to these cafés to connect to the Internet and play games online. In addition, Stockholm was one of the first cities to introduce new technology to replace Wi-Fi. This technology will allow people to access the Internet more quickly. ___

☐ a. In conclusion, Taipei is a world leader in technology.
☐ b. In summary, accessing the Internet in Stockholm is simple.
☐ c. For this reason, Internet cafés are very popular with teenagers.
☐ d. For these reasons, Stockholm will likely be a world leader in Internet technology in the future.
☐ e. In conclusion, you do not need to worry about a connection to the Internet if you visit Stockholm.
☐ f. To summarize, buying a computer in Sweden can be expensive.

D. Skill Quiz

Check (✓) the correct answer for each item.

1 The concluding sentence is usually located
- ☐ a. at the beginning of a paragraph.
- ☐ b. in the middle of a paragraph.
- ☐ c. at the end of a paragraph.

2 A concluding sentence often
- ☐ a. restates the main idea.
- ☐ b. introduces the main idea.
- ☐ c. introduces new information about the main idea.

3 A concluding sentence may
- ☐ a. give examples.
- ☐ b. offer a suggestion.
- ☐ c. introduce a new topic.

4 A concluding sentence sometimes
- ☐ a. asks a question.
- ☐ b. makes a prediction.
- ☐ c. changes the controlling idea.

5 Choose the best concluding sentence for this topic sentence: *Training programs help people learn Internet skills.*
- ☐ a. In summary, take a training course to improve your Internet skills.
- ☐ b. In summary, one way to improve Internet skills is through books.
- ☐ c. In summary, it is a good idea to be on time for training classes.

6 Choose the best concluding sentence for this topic sentence: *Businesses in Tokyo must have Wi-Fi to be successful.*
- ☐ a. To conclude, do not use the Wi-Fi at work for personal reasons in Tokyo.
- ☐ b. To conclude, it is not expensive for businesses in Tokyo to provide Wi-Fi.
- ☐ c. To conclude, a business in Tokyo probably will not succeed if it does not use Wi-Fi.

7 Choose the best concluding sentence for this topic sentence: *New technology is expensive, but devices get cheaper over time.*
- ☐ a. For these reasons, modern gadgets get cheaper every year.
- ☐ b. For these reasons, Internet cafés are popular places to play video games cheaply.
- ☐ c. For these reasons, expensive devices can be purchased with a credit card.

8 Choose the best concluding sentence for this topic sentence: *Smartphones may replace cameras.*
- ☐ a. In conclusion, some people also like using tablet computers.
- ☐ b. In conclusion, smartphones will come in a variety of colors.
- ☐ c. In conclusion, cameras may not exist in the future because people will use phones instead.

9 Choose the best concluding sentence for this topic sentence: *Some psychologists are concerned about how long children spend on the Internet at school.*
- ☐ a. In summary, children clearly play too many computer games.
- ☐ b. To conclude, parents should limit the time children spend outdoors.
- ☐ c. In the future, schools may look for ways to decrease Internet use.

10 Choose the best concluding sentence for this topic sentence: *Students need to be cautious when doing research online.*
- ☐ a. For this reason, encyclopedias will become less popular over time.
- ☐ b. For this reason, it is likely that colleges will offer more and more guidance in effective Internet use.
- ☐ c. For this reason, most professors will advise students not to read books.

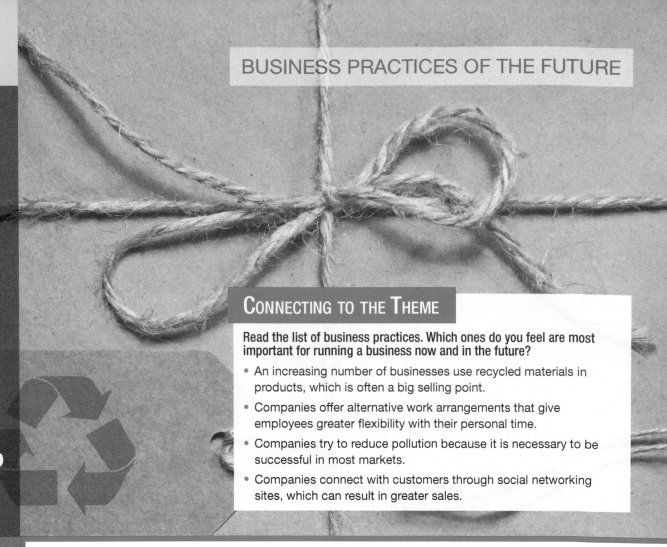

6

Avoiding Sentence Fragments

BUSINESS PRACTICES OF THE FUTURE

CONNECTING TO THE THEME

Read the list of business practices. Which ones do you feel are most important for running a business now and in the future?

- An increasing number of businesses use recycled materials in products, which is often a big selling point.
- Companies offer alternative work arrangements that give employees greater flexibility with their personal time.
- Companies try to reduce pollution because it is necessary to be successful in most markets.
- Companies connect with customers through social networking sites, which can result in greater sales.

A. Skill Presentation

A complete sentence has a subject and a verb and expresses a complete idea. A **sentence fragment** is missing either a subject or a verb, so it does not express a complete idea and should be avoided. Here are two examples of sentence fragments.

Want to help the environment. ✗   (This sentence has no subject.)
Sustainability very important. ✗   (This sentence has no verb.)

Some verbs require an auxiliary verb like *be*, *do*, or *have*. If this verb is missing, the sentence is incomplete. The sentence below is a fragment because the auxiliary verb *is* is missing. When it's added, it becomes a complete sentence.

BoMart collecting old bottles to make tote bags. ✗
BoMart is collecting old bottles to make tote bags. ✓

A dependent clause begins with a subordinating conjunction like *because*, *if*, *when*, *before*, *after*, *that*, *which*, or *who*. A dependent clause by itself is a sentence fragment. It must be connected with an independent clause to make a complete sentence. The sentence below is a dependent clause that does not express a complete idea. It is therefore a sentence fragment. It needs to be connected with an independent clause to express a complete idea.

Because it helps the company and the planet. ✗
Because it helps the company and the planet, recycling is a good idea. ✓

B. Over to You

1 **Read the sentence fragments and decide what is missing. Write *S* for Subject or *V* for Verb / Auxiliary Verb.**

___ **1** Is good for business.

___ **2** Companies using sustainable practices.

2 **Read each item in the chart. Decide if it is a sentence fragment or not. Check (✓) the box in the correct column.**

	SENTENCE FRAGMENT	COMPLETE SENTENCE
1. If it helps the company in many ways, too.		
2. I like companies that care about the environment.		
3. There is no risk because the business is reliable.		
4. Before they take advantage of new business ideas.		

3 **Find and check (✓) six sentence fragments.**

☐ a. Social media offer companies two options.
☐ b. If they want to advertise on social networking websites.
☐ c. Companies can pay for advertisements or use free services to show their products.
☐ d. Our company trying both.
☐ e. We are paying for ads on several websites.
☐ f. We also creating free pages on social networking sites.
☐ g. Both kinds of advertising are valuable.
☐ h. Both ways help cut costs.
☐ i. Now are planning new ways to advertise online.
☐ j. The company uses video conferences for meetings.
☐ k. Will help us increase sales.
☐ l. Which is good for the company.

CHECK!

1 A _____ _____ is incomplete and a mistake. It does not include a subject and a complete verb.

2 A sentence with a _____ clause but without an _____ clause is also a sentence fragment.

C. Practice

1 Read each item in the chart. Decide if it is a sentence fragment or not. If it is, decide on the reason and check (✓) the box in the correct column.

	COMPLETE SENTENCE	NO SUBJECT (SENTENCE FRAGMENT)	NO VERB OR NO AUXILIARY VERB (SENTENCE FRAGMENT)	DEPENDENT CLAUSE (SENTENCE FRAGMENT)
1. Are allowing employees to work from home.				
2. Many of his co-workers work from home.				
3. Some employees keeping in touch through video conferences.				
4. Because e-mail is so fast.				
5. Sometimes is difficult to manage employees online.				
6. Employees share information on secure sites.				
7. If they do not have to compete with other employees.				
8. Employees at this company their computers every day.				
9. Offices are becoming smaller.				
10. When the office is open.				

2 Read the sentences. Circle *CS* for Complete Sentence or *SF* for Sentence Fragment. Then decide what is missing. Write *S* for Subject, *V* for Verb / Auxiliary Verb, or *IC* for Independent Clause.

CS | SF   **1** Modern software is helping companies with international communication. ___

CS | SF   **2** Because computers will be able to work much faster. ___

CS | SF   **3** Businesses new technology for salespeople's benefit. ___

CS | SF   **4** Who take advantage of online resources for video conferences. ___

CS | SF   **5** Helps businesses create new ways to reach customers. ___

CS | SF   **6** They still work after most people have gone home. ___

CS | SF   **7** Companies been using online surveys for many years. ___

CS | SF   **8** When they want to take advantage of new ways to share information. ___

CS | SF   **9** Currently, is working outside of the office two days a week. ___

CS | SF   **10** That they consider spending so much money on advertising. ___

D. Skill Quiz

Check (✓) the correct answer for each item.

1 A complete sentence must have
   - a. a subject and a verb.
   - b. an adjective and a verb.
   - c. a dependent clause and a subject.

2 A sentence that is not complete is
   - a. an independent clause.
   - b. a sentence fragment.
   - c. a complex sentence.

3 A dependent clause is a sentence fragment if it
   - a. has a subject and a verb.
   - b. is not connected with an independent clause.
   - c. expresses more than one complete idea.

4 *Technology will help businesses reach customers and increase sales.*
   This is a
   - a. complete sentence.
   - b. sentence fragment. It needs a verb or an auxiliary verb.
   - c. sentence fragment. It needs an independent clause.

5 *Because it is less expensive than traditional marketing.*
   This is a
   - a. complete sentence.
   - b. sentence fragment. It needs a verb or an auxiliary verb.
   - c. sentence fragment. It needs an independent clause.

6 *Many people working outside of the office sometimes.*
   This is a sentence fragment because
   - a. it needs a subject.
   - b. it needs a verb or an auxiliary verb.
   - c. it needs an independent clause.

7 *Nowadays, work from home one or two days per week.*
   This is a sentence fragment because
   - a. it needs a subject.
   - b. it needs a verb or an auxiliary verb.
   - c. it needs an independent clause.

8 Choose the word that will make this fragment a complete sentence: *Our company ___ trying different ways of advertising.*
   - a. they
   - b. by
   - c. is

9 Choose the word that will make this fragment a complete sentence: *___ are more useful than other ways of collecting data.*
   - a. Surveys
   - b. Have
   - c. Because

10 Choose the words that will make this fragment a complete sentence: *___ when they feel confident.*
   - a. The managers at this company
   - b. Employees may work harder
   - c. Because they are more successful

LEARNING HOW TO REMEMBER

Avoiding Run-Ons and Comma Splices

CONNECTING TO THE THEME

How much do you know about memory? Are these statements true or false?

1 There are four kinds of memory, and they are not related.

2 Short-term memory helps us forget a small amount of information for a short time.

3 Most people can remember only about seven pieces of information for 30 seconds.

4 Long-term memory helps us hold memories for a lifetime.

5 When new information is used often, it doesn't stay in our memory as long.

1 False (there are two types of memory, and they are related), 2 False (it helps us remember information), 3 True, 4 True, 5 False (it stays longer in our memory).

A. Skill Presentation

A sentence can have one or more independent clauses. Look at this sentence. Notice that the two independent clauses are connected by a comma and the conjunction *and*. Some common conjunctions are *and*, *but*, *or*, and *so*. Always put a comma before the conjunction.

Maria studied for an important test, **and** she memorized facts for a presentation.

A **run-on sentence** has two or more independent clauses that are missing a comma, a conjunction, or both a comma and a conjunction. Look at this run-on sentence. There are two independent clauses, but there is no comma and no conjunction. To correct this, a comma and conjunction must be added.

One kind is short-term memory the other kind is long-term memory. ✗
One kind is short-term memory, **and** the other kind is long-term memory. ✓

A **comma splice** is one kind of run-on sentence. It has two or more independent clauses joined by a comma, but it does not have a conjunction. Look at this comma splice. There are two independent clauses and there is a comma, but there is no conjunction. To correct this, a conjunction must be added.

Some people want better long-term memory, others want better short-term memory. ✗
Some people want better long-term memory, **but** others want better short-term memory. ✓

B. Over to You

1 Check (✓) five items that are run-on sentences or comma splices.

☐ a. A lot of people struggle with memory problems, but the right diet might help their forgetfulness.

☐ b. Research shows certain foods can boost brain power they may be a good addition to your diet.

☐ c. Blueberries are a good choice for many people.

☐ d. Eating them daily may improve memory function.

☐ e. Fatty acids are crucial to brain health, they can be found in fish and nuts.

☐ f. It is a good idea to add salmon or tuna to your menu twice a week you can try eating walnuts, too.

☐ g. Many red foods can also help with memory function, so some people suggest eating tomatoes and strawberries.

☐ h. What people drink also plays a part in memory improvement, some experts say water is the best choice.

☐ i. Coffee can help with concentration in small amounts too much coffee can hurt.

☐ j. These diet tips can be effective for people wanting to improve their memories.

2 Read the sentences. Write *C* for Correct, *RS* for Run-On Sentence, or *CS* for Comma Splice.

___ 1 Max studied for the exam but he could not remember the answers.

___ 2 My sister has a lot of friends, she always remembers their names.

___ 3 Felix has a fantastic long-term memory, but he can't always remember things at first.

___ 4 We studied very hard for the test, we forgot everything on the day of the test for some reason.

___ 5 Although memory is a natural skill, it can also be improved.

___ 6 Some people concentrate better in a quiet room others prefer a little noise.

___ 7 Daniel struggles with his work, he needs a better study routine.

CHECK!

1 A _____ _____ has two or more independent clauses connected with no comma, no conjunction, or neither a comma nor a conjunction.

2 A _____ _____ has two or more independent clauses connected only with a comma.

C. Practice

1 Read each sentence in the chart. Decide if it is a run-on sentence, a comma splice, or correct. Check (✓) the box in the correct column.

	RUN-ON SENTENCE	COMMA SPLICE	CORRECT
1. Many students struggle to recall facts, and they need advice about how to remember better.			
2. Sara went to a presentation she learned ways to improve her memory.			
3. The expert gave advice about when to do assignments, he gave advice about memorizing facts.			
4. You should use information in a variety of ways, or you will rapidly forget it.			
5. Short-term memory holds a small amount of information long-term memory holds much more.			
6. Short-term memories can become long-term memories, using information frequently helps.			
7. I need to improve my concentration so I turn off the TV when I do homework.			
8. He has to give a presentation tomorrow, and he cannot recall where he left his notes.			

2 Read the sentences. Circle *C* for Correct Sentence or *I* for Incorrect Sentence. Then write *RS* for Run-On Sentence or *CS* for Comma Splice.

C | I   **1** It is not difficult to improve your memory, but you have to practice. ___

C | I   **2** A good memory helps you learn better it is a good idea to improve your memorization skills. ___

C | I   **3** Brain games are fun to play, they help improve concentration. ___

C | I   **4** Research shows that chewing gum may help people remember new information, my advice is to chew sugar-free gum. ___

C | I   **5** One study showed that fish oil helped school children's memories it also improved their behavior at school. ___

C | I   **6** A heavy meal can hurt your concentration, but small healthy meals can boost your brain power. ___

C | I   **7** You can repeat information aloud to help remember it, you can write it down. ___

C | I   **8** It is important to stay alert you should take a study break every hour. ___

D. Skill Quiz

Check (✓) the correct answer for each item.

1 An independent clause
  - a. expresses an incomplete idea.
  - b. expresses a complete idea.
  - c. has no subject and no verb.

2 One example of a run-on sentence is a sentence with
  - a. two independent clauses and no comma.
  - b. two independent clauses, a comma, and a conjunction.
  - c. one independent clause and several commas.

3 A comma splice is usually missing
  - a. a verb.
  - b. a comma.
  - c. a conjunction.

4 Choose the comma splice.
  - a. Puzzles are fun to do. They can help exercise your brain.
  - b. Puzzles are fun to do, they can help exercise your brain.
  - c. Puzzles are fun to do they can help exercise your brain.

5 Choose the comma splice.
  - a. Fish oil is good for brain health, you should eat fish every week.
  - b. Fish oil is good for brain health, so you should eat fish every week.
  - c. Fish oil is good for brain health. You should eat fish every week.

6 Choose the run-on sentence.
  - a. Blueberries can improve memory function, and they are also tasty.
  - b. Blueberries can improve memory function and they are also tasty.
  - c. Blueberries can improve memory function, they are also tasty.

7 Choose the run-on sentence.
  - a. People should drink plenty of water, but they should not drink too much coffee.
  - b. People should drink plenty of water, they should not drink too much coffee.
  - c. People should drink plenty of water they should not drink too much coffee.

8 Choose the run-on sentence.
  - a. I have to give a presentation later I don't remember when.
  - b. I have to give a presentation later, I don't remember when.
  - c. I have to give a presentation later, but I don't remember when.

9 Choose the correct sentence.
  - a. Short-term memory helps you remember where you parked your car this information will not usually go into long-term memory.
  - b. Short-term memory helps you remember where you parked your car, but this information will not usually go into long-term memory.
  - c. Short-term memory helps you remember where you parked your car, this information will not usually go into long-term memory.

10 Choose the correct sentence.
  - a. He heard the advice about memory improvement, and he wants to become less forgetful.
  - b. He heard the advice about memory improvement he wants to become less forgetful.
  - c. He heard the advice about memory improvement, he wants to become less forgetful.

COMPUTERS AND CRIME

A. Skill Presentation

Use **parallel structure** in lists of **words**, phrases, or clauses to make sentences flow well. Sentences without parallel structure can sound awkward and may be incorrect. Look at this example. It has parallel structure with words. All the words in the list are nouns (*children*, *preteens*, and *teenagers*).

Cyber bullying is a serious problem for **children**, **preteens**, and **teenagers**.

Now look at this example. It has parallel structure with phrases. Both phrases are prepositional phrases that start with the preposition *on*.

This includes sending malicious messages on computers or on smartphones.

Next, look at this example. It has parallel structure with clauses. Both clauses start with *that*.

Experts say that passwords should be long and that computers should have virus protection software.

Finally, look at an example that does not have parallel structure. *A problem* does not follow the same pattern as *hurtful* and *dangerous*. *A problem* is a noun, but *hurtful* and *dangerous* are adjectives. To give the sentence parallel structure, all the words should be the same part of speech.

Cyber bullying is hurtful, dangerous, and a problem. ✗
Cyber bullying is hurtful, dangerous, and mean. ✓

B. Over to You

1   Check (✓) the sentences that have parallel structure.

1   ☐   a. Create a password that is long and that contains numbers.
     ☐   b. Create a password that is long and by using numbers.
     ☐   c. Create a password that is long with numbers.

2   ☐   a. Cyber bullies are usually hurtful and people who have low self-confidence.
     ☐   b. Cyber bullies are usually people with low self-confidence and who want to hurt others.
     ☐   c. Cyber bullies are usually people who have low self-confidence and who want to hurt others.

3   ☐   a. The number of cyber bullies is increasing and has caused problems in many schools.
     ☐   b. The number of cyber bullies is increasing and is causing problems in many schools.
     ☐   c. The number of cyber bullies is increasing and is dangerous.

2   Match each sentence beginning (1–7) with the correct sentence ending (a–g) to make sentences with parallel structure.

___   1   Computer hacking is serious,

___   2   Cyber bullying is a growing problem

___   3   We took a computer class to practice what we know,

___   4   Hackers access personal computers,

___   5   I learned how to use my smartphone by reading the manual,

___   6   Cyber bullies send malicious messages on cell phones,

___   7   Cyber bullying is a problem that can affect children,

a   and a serious crime.

b   that can cause emotional pain, and that can become serious.

c   to improve our abilities, and to learn new skills.

d   malicious, and illegal.

e   steal credit card information, and figure out passwords.

f   on the Internet, and on smartphones.

g   by looking up information online, and by asking a friend for help.

CHECK!

1   Use parallel structure in lists of words, phrases, or _____ to make your sentence flow well.

2   To be sure your sentence has parallel structure, use ____ ____ word patterns when you write lists.

C. Practice

1 Read each sentence in the chart. Decide if it has parallel structure or not. Check (✓) the box in the correct column.

	PARALLEL STRUCTURE	NOT PARALLEL STRUCTURE
1. The latest smartphones are fast, powerful, and small.		
2. The latest smartphones are popular, in stores, and useful.		
3. Cyber bullies can be mean, scary, and should be punished.		
4. Cyber bullies can be hurtful, annoying, and cruel.		
5. Hackers access information, create viruses, and shut down communication.		
6. Hackers stole passwords, can create computer programs, and may have taken information illegally.		
7. To prevent hackers, I use special software and with strong passwords.		
8. I prevent hackers by choosing creative passwords and by purchasing anti-virus software.		
9. They plan to sell programs that will stop viruses and to discourage hackers.		

2 Circle the correct words or phrases to make sentences with parallel structure.

1 Hackers break into e-mail accounts, *computer systems,* | *by stealing,* | *are common*, and wireless devices.

2 Hackers cause problems for hospitals, government offices, and *banks* | *are illegal* | *by taking important information.*

3 Hacking is *mean,* | *a crime,* | *to steal*, dangerous, and illegal.

4 In the United States, the Federal Bureau of Investigation studies, *investigates,* | *can investigate,* | *is investigating*, and stops computer crimes.

5 Many cyber criminals send e-mails to people asking for a check, a money transfer, or *cash* | *to take their money* | *that they need cash.*

6 An e-mail may say a person needs money because his credit cards were stolen or *because his passport is missing* | *his passport* | *if he loses his passport.*

7 The cyber criminal hopes that people will be kind and *to send him money* | *for sending him money* | *that they will send him money.*

8 The cyber criminal does not return the money. He uses it for travel, *with* | *for* | *by* shopping, or for other personal items.

9 You can report e-mails *that* | *to* | *can* seem fake and that seem dangerous.

D. Skill Quiz

Check (✓) the correct answer for each item.

1 Parallel structure means using ____ word patterns in lists.

☐ a. different
☐ b. similar
☐ c. various

2 Use parallel structure in lists of words, phrases, and

☐ a. paragraphs.
☐ b. sentences.
☐ c. clauses.

3 Choose the option that gives this sentence parallel structure: *Hacking is a serious, dangerous, and ____ crime.*

☐ a. to worry about
☐ b. against the law
☐ c. malicious

4 Choose the option that gives this sentence parallel structure: *Cyber criminals lie, cheat, and ____.*

☐ a. steal
☐ b. theft
☐ c. may be malicious

5 Choose the option that gives this sentence parallel structure: *Be careful of e-mails that ask for money and ____ from someone you do not know.*

☐ a. are coming
☐ b. that come
☐ c. can be

6 Choose the option that gives this sentence parallel structure: *Cyber criminals can be punished ____ and by the police.*

☐ a. by the FBI
☐ b. for some crimes
☐ c. if the crimes are severe

7 Choose the sentence with parallel structure.

☐ a. The FBI hopes to catch people who create scams and when they are hacking into computers.
☐ b. The FBI hopes to catch people who create scams and if they hack into computers.
☐ c. The FBI hopes to catch people who create scams and who hack into computers.

8 Choose the sentence with parallel structure.

☐ a. Children should tell an adult if they get an e-mail that is unwanted or threatening.
☐ b. Children should tell an adult if they get an e-mail that is unwanted or contains threats.
☐ c. Children should tell an adult if they get an e-mail they do not want or feel threatened.

9 Choose the sentence with parallel structure.

☐ a. Only accept e-mails from teachers, from friends, and that someone in your family sends.
☐ b. Only accept e-mails from teachers, from friends, and from family.
☐ c. Only accept e-mails from teachers, from friends, and the ones your family sends.

10 Choose the sentence with parallel structure.

☐ a. Cyber criminals include people who send fake e-mails, who bully others, and who hack into computers.
☐ b. Cyber criminals include people who send fake e-mails, bullies, and who hack into computers.
☐ c. Cyber criminals include people who send fake e-mails, by texting, and with computers.

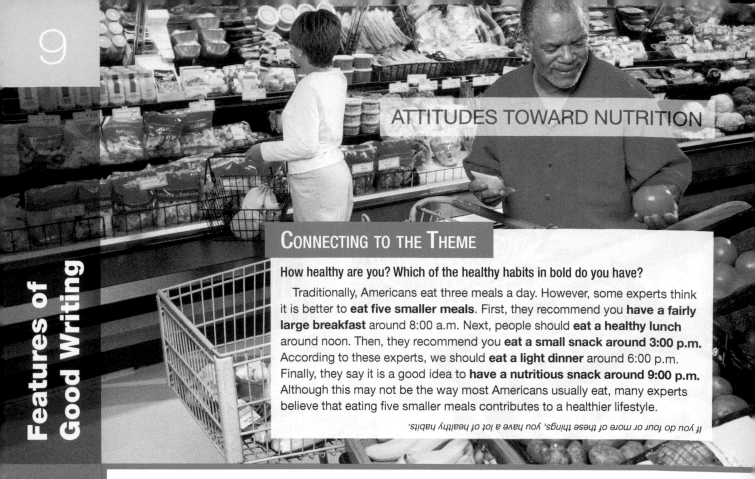

9

Features of Good Writing

CONNECTING TO THE THEME

How healthy are you? Which of the healthy habits in bold do you have?

Traditionally, Americans eat three meals a day. However, some experts think it is better to **eat five smaller meals**. First, they recommend you **have a fairly large breakfast** around 8:00 a.m. Next, people should **eat a healthy lunch** around noon. Then, they recommend you **eat a small snack around 3:00 p.m.** According to these experts, we should **eat a light dinner** around 6:00 p.m. Finally, they say it is a good idea to **have a nutritious snack around 9:00 p.m.** Although this may not be the way most Americans usually eat, many experts believe that eating five smaller meals contributes to a healthier lifestyle.

If you do four or more of these things, you have a lot of healthy habits.

A. Skill Presentation

One feature of good writing is that it has a **clear purpose**. When you write academic paragraphs, your purpose is often to inform readers about something new or to persuade readers what to do or what to think. The purpose of this paragraph is to inform readers about healthy times to eat meals.

TRANSITION WORDS

TIME ORDER

FORMAL LANGUAGE

DETAILS

Some experts think it is better to eat five smaller meals. First, they recommend eating a large breakfast around 8:00 a.m. Second, experts recommend eating a healthy lunch around noon. Third, experts suggest eating a small snack, like fruit, around 3:00 p.m. An appropriate time for dinner is around 6:00 p.m. Having a healthy snack around 9:00 p.m. may also be beneficial. Some experts believe that several small meals lead to a healthier lifestyle.

A second feature of good writing is that it relates to a **specific audience**. When you write academic paragraphs, your audience is often your teacher or your classmates. Often, teachers will expect to read formal writing that uses the third person. This paragraph uses formal language, such as *experts*, and the third person (*they*).

A third feature of good writing is **clarity**. Readers should be able to understand your writing and not be confused. Including words that give detail can help add clarity to your writing. This paragraph has clarity because it gives details to make the ideas clear.

A fourth feature of good writing is that it is **coherent**, or clearly organized. For example, paragraphs can be in time order or in the order of importance. Transition words and transition phrases can help make your writing more coherent. The sentences in this paragraph are in time order, and there are transition words that help add coherence.

B. Over to You

1 **Check (✓) the paragraph that has more features of good writing.**

☐ a. Traditionally, Americans eat three meals a day. To start, they may only have time to eat a small amount of food for breakfast. Many people eat a bagel or have a small bowl of cereal around 7:00 a.m. Next, Americans typically eat lunch around noon. Lunch is often a small meal like a sandwich or a bowl of soup. Finally, many Americans have a large dinner around 6:00 p.m. This often includes a variety of food. Everyone is different, but many Americans follow a similar pattern.

☐ b. Traditionally, Americans eat three meals a day. They eat lunch in the afternoon. Lunch is often small. I usually grab a quick bite in the morning. I think everyone should eat a healthy breakfast. My favorite breakfast food is cereal. Many Americans have a big dinner. This often includes a whole bunch of food. Everyone is different, but we usually follow this pattern.

2 **Read the paragraph and answer the questions below using the options given. There are four extra options.**

The United States Department of Agriculture (USDA) is an important government agency that deals with food. There are ten different departments in the USDA. Each department has a specific responsibility. For example, the Food and Nutrition Service (FNS) makes sure that food in the United States is safe. It also educates people about nutrition. In summary, the USDA helps inform people about a wide variety of food issues.

a teacher or a professor   *about nutrition*   **important, specific, wide**
In summary   **the writer's close friends**   *USDA, FNS, United States*
to compare the USDA to the FNS   **to inform readers about what the USDA does**

1 What is the author's purpose for writing this paragraph?

_____

2 The audience for this paragraph is probably:

_____

3 Which words add clarity to this paragraph?

_____

4 Which phrase helps make this paragraph more coherent?

_____

CHECK!

1 Good writing has a clear _____, or the reason you are writing.
2 It relates to an _____, such as a teacher or classmates.
3 It has _____, so that your readers understand all of your ideas.
4 It is _____ because it is clearly organized and may include transition words or phrases.

C. Practice

1 Read each pair of sentences. Decide which sentence in the pair has more clarity and which sentence has less clarity. Write *MC* for More Clarity or *LC* for Less Clarity.

1 ___ a. Many people eat food on the weekends.
   ___ b. Many Americans eat brunch on the weekends.

2 ___ a. People eat brunch around 11:00, which is after a typical breakfast but before a typical lunch.
   ___ b. Brunch is a meal that people eat between two other mealtimes.

3 ___ a. Pancakes are a typical food for brunch, and people almost always have coffee or orange juice.
   ___ b. Pancakes are served at some meals, and people may have different kinds of drinks.

4 ___ a. Young people go out for meals together.
   ___ b. Young people often go to restaurant brunches in large groups.

5 ___ a. Some restaurants have weekend brunch specials with a main dish, smaller dishes, and coffee for approximately $15.
   ___ b. Some restaurants have brunch specials where you get a lot of food for one price.

2 Number the sentences in the correct order to form a coherent paragraph.

The USDA recommends a number of steps to ensure that chicken is handled safely.

___ Finally, use the chicken in one or two days.

___ Chicken can go bad after that, and it can be very dangerous for your health.

___ Second, put chicken in a plastic bag after you buy it.

___ First, make sure chicken is cold before you buy it.

___ As soon as you get home, put the chicken in the refrigerator right away.

Follow these tips to be sure you are handling chicken properly.

D. Skill Quiz

Check (✓) the correct answer for each item.

1 *To inform* and *to persuade* are
- [ ] a. common purposes for writing.
- [ ] b. typical transition phrases.
- [ ] c. ideas to increase clarity.

2 To give a paragraph clarity
- [ ] a. think about who will read it.
- [ ] b. use words with detail to make ideas clearer.
- [ ] c. add transition words throughout the paragraph.

3 A coherent paragraph has sentences in
- [ ] a. an order that makes sense, such as time order.
- [ ] b. the order of length, with shorter sentences first.
- [ ] c. an order that challenges the audience.

4 An academic paragraph does not use
- [ ] a. formal language.
- [ ] b. informal language.
- [ ] c. the third person (*they*).

5 Which sentence's purpose is to give information?
- [ ] a. In my opinion, it is crucial for farmers to work with the FSA.
- [ ] b. The FSA should increase their programs to help more farmers.
- [ ] c. The FSA is a department in the USDA that assists farmers.

6 Which sentence's purpose is to persuade?
- [ ] a. Some Americans eat three meals a day, but others eat five or six.
- [ ] b. According to experts, there are many ways to improve your health.
- [ ] c. It is important to eat five meals a day in order to lose weight.

7 Which sentence uses the most detail to give it clarity?
- [ ] a. One government agency says people should eat five meals.
- [ ] b. An agency thinks people should eat food at different times.
- [ ] c. The FNS recommends eating five nutritious meals each day.

8 Which sentence uses the most detail to give it clarity?
- [ ] a. The FNS provides healthy food to disadvantaged children.
- [ ] b. There is a service in the United States that gives food to children.
- [ ] c. The FNS provides food for people.

9 Which sentences use a transition word to help add coherence?
- [ ] a. There are many things you can do to be healthy. Eat nutritional food and exercise regularly.
- [ ] b. There are many things you can do to be healthy. First, eat food with high nutritional value.
- [ ] c. You can be healthier by eating food with high nutritional value. You'll be happier, as well.

10 Which sentences are in an order that makes them coherent?
- [ ] a. First, make sure the vegetables are fresh. Next, put them in a plastic bag before you buy them.
- [ ] b. Next, wash the vegetables under cold running water. To start, make sure the vegetables are fresh.
- [ ] c. Finally, steam the vegetables or cook them with olive oil. Then put them in a plastic bag before you buy them.

Clarity in Sentences and Paragraphs

COLOR

CONNECTING TO THE THEME

What feelings are associated with colors in these countries? Match the colors and countries with their meanings.

a danger   **b** purity   **c** death   **d** luck

1 In Japan, Europe, and the U.S., red can signal ___. People in those countries use red in warning signs.

2 In China, red represents ___. This color is used in New Year's decorations to bring good fortune in the new year.

3 According to one article, in the U.S. and Europe, white means ___. White is a popular choice for painting bathrooms and health spas.

4 In China and Japan, white is often associated with ___. This color may be used in times of mourning.

1a, 2d, 3b, 4c

A. Skill Presentation

There are three ways to improve the **clarity** of your writing. One way is to use language that is specific, not vague or general. Use **specific adjectives** to add more information. Avoid common words like *good*, *great*, *nice*, and *bad* – these are too general and do not help make ideas clearer. Look at this sentence. To improve clarity, we could change *good* to a word like *skilled* – a more vivid and specific adjective.

She is ~~good~~ **skilled** at choosing colors for websites.

A second way to improve clarity is to use **pronouns** carefully. A pronoun that refers to a noun in a previous sentence may be confusing. If it is not completely clear what a pronoun refers to, change it to a specific noun or noun phrase. Look at this sentence. What Laura enjoys is not completely clear. The pronoun *it* might refer to *the cross-cultural impact of color*, to *does research*, or to *an event*. To improve clarity, we could change it to a specific noun or noun phrase, like *learning about cross-cultural differences*.

Laura does research on the cross-cultural impact of color before **she** plans an event. **She** enjoys ~~it~~ **learning about cross-cultural differences**.

A third way to add clarity to your writing is to use **action verbs** instead of *to be* as the main verbs. This makes the sentence more specific, helps the reader understand meaning, and makes your writing more interesting. Be careful – sometimes when you replace a form of *to be* with an action verb, you may need to rephrase the sentence. Look at this sentence. To improve clarity, we could change *was careful* to an action verb phrase like *made careful decisions*.

He did not want to offend his hosts, so he ~~was~~ / **made** careful decisions about choosing colors for business gifts.

B. Over to You

1 Read the sentences. Choose the word in bold that should be changed to improve clarity. Write A, B, or C.

____ **1** ^A**Many** people feel that it is not ^B**nice** to wear ^C**black** to a wedding.

____ **2** White ^A**flowers** might be inappropriate in some situations. ^B**They** may be considered ^C**unlucky**.

____ **3** Selecting appropriate ^A**colors** for ^B**global** websites ^C**is** time consuming.

2 Look at each pair of sentences. Sentence *a* is not very clear. Sentence *b* is clearer. Decide what change the writer made to improve it. Write *P/N* if the writer replaced an unclear pronoun with a specific noun. Write *V* if the writer changed the verb *to be* to an action verb.

1 a. Children tend to prefer purple and orange more than adults do. They often choose these colors for bedroom decorations.

____ b. Children tend to prefer purple and orange more than adults do. Children often choose these colors for bedroom decorations.

2 a. Green has a positive effect on people's emotions. This is why hospitals often have light green rooms.

____ b. Green has a positive effect on people's emotions. This explains why hospitals often have light green rooms.

3 a. Red can be a problem in some situations. Schools often avoid this color in classrooms because it has an overwhelming effect on children.

____ b. Red can create a problem in some situations. Schools often avoid this color in classrooms because it has an overwhelming effect on children.

4 a. Women are more likely than men to have a favorite color. In addition, they usually prefer soft hues.

____ b. Women are more likely than men to have a favorite color. In addition, women usually prefer soft hues.

5 a. A successful delivery company uses a shade of brown for its trucks. It can suggest reliability in North American culture.

____ b. A successful delivery company uses a shade of brown for its trucks. The color brown can suggest reliability in North American culture.

6 a. Women are generally more knowledgeable about color names than men are. Current research supports this conclusion.

____ b. Women generally know more color names than men do. Current research supports this conclusion.

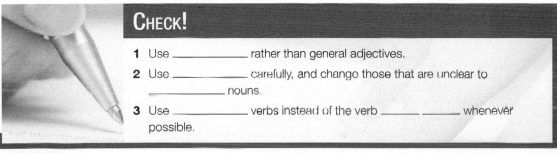

CHECK!

1 Use _____ rather than general adjectives.

2 Use _____ carefully, and change those that are unclear to _____ nouns.

3 Use _____ verbs instead of the verb _____ _____ whenever possible.

C. Practice

1 **Circle the correct clearer, more specific words to replace the words in bold for each item.**

good | significant

1 The color red is often used on signs because it has a **big** impact on the people who view it.

safe | stimulating

2 Some experts believe that the color orange has a **good** effect on diners' appetites.

negative | rude

3 A 2010 study showed that some cultures have a **bad** reaction to brown and orange.

plays an important role | is useful

4 Color choice **is important** in global marketing.

good | safe

5 Culture experts say that yellow is a **fine** choice for gift giving in Asia.

People in different cultures | Colors

6 People in different cultures view colors in different ways. **They** can be considered lucky or unlucky, depending on where you are.

The color green | Food packaging

7 Green is used more than blue in food packaging. **It** often signifies something "healthy" or "natural."

Royalty | This color

8 Purple often signifies "royalty" in the West. **It** was the choice of kings and queens in the Middle Ages.

produces calm feelings | seems nice

9 According to Western psychology, blue **is calming** for many people.

create | do

10 Mixing two hues can **make** a third color.

2 **Read each pair of sentences, and check (✓) the one that is clearest. Then circle the words that were changed to improve it.**

1 ☐ a. Some students associate words with colors. This helps them remember them better.
☐ b. Some students associate words with colors. This helps them remember the words better.

2 ☐ a. The Olympics logo has five rings. The logo consists of five colors: red, yellow, green, blue, and black.
☐ b. The Olympics logo has five rings. The logo is five colors: red, yellow, green, blue, and black.

3 ☐ a. The white dress for American and European brides is a relatively recent tradition. This fashion started in the nineteenth century.
☐ b. The white dress for American and European brides is a relatively new tradition. This fashion started in the nineteenth century.

4 ☐ a. Brides wear red or pink in India. These colors are the most popular.
☐ b. Brides wear red or pink in India. Most brides choose these colors.

5 ☐ a. Black represents death and mourning in Western cultures. It is often associated with negative emotions.
☐ b. Black represents death and mourning in Western cultures. Black is often associated with negative emotions.

D. Skill Quiz

Check (✓) the correct answer for each item.

1 Clarity is how easy it is to
- [ ] a. understand a piece of writing.
- [ ] b. write a paragraph.
- [ ] c. revise a piece of writing.

2 One way to improve clarity is to replace ___ with a more specific one.
- [ ] a. a complicated verb
- [ ] b. a coordinating conjunction
- [ ] c. a common adjective

3 Another way to improve clarity is to change ___ to a specific noun.
- [ ] a. an unclear pronoun
- [ ] b. an indirect object
- [ ] c. a proper noun

4 Another way to improve clarity is to replace ___ with an action verb.
- [ ] a. the subject
- [ ] b. the verb *to be*
- [ ] c. every verb

5 Choose the sentence with the most clarity.
- [ ] a. Red and gold are nice colors in some cultures.
- [ ] b. Red and gold are good colors in some cultures.
- [ ] c. Red and gold are considered lucky colors in some cultures.

6 Choose the sentence with the most clarity.
- [ ] a. Women are typically better than them at naming colors.
- [ ] b. Women are typically better than men at naming colors.
- [ ] c. Women are typically better than him at naming colors.

7 Choose the sentence with the most clarity.
- [ ] a. Choosing colors for a global website is very hard.
- [ ] b. Choosing colors for a global website presents a serious challenge.
- [ ] c. Choosing colors for a global website is extremely difficult.

8 A: *In some cultures, people believe that white is bad luck.*
B: *In some cultures, people believe that white represents bad luck.*
What makes sentence B clearer than sentence A?
- [ ] a. A specific adjective replaces a common adjective.
- [ ] b. A specific noun replaces a pronoun.
- [ ] c. A specific verb replaces *to be*.

9 A: *Red represents luck. For this reason, it appears in New Year's decorations.*
B: *Red represents luck. For this reason, this color appears in New Year's decorations.*
What makes sentence B clearer than sentence A?
- [ ] a. A specific adjective replaces a common adjective.
- [ ] b. A specific noun replaces a pronoun.
- [ ] c. A specific verb replaces *to be*.

10 A: *Good global advertisers study the cultures where they want to do business.*
B: *Successful global advertisers study the cultures where they want to do business.*
What makes sentence B clearer than sentence A?
- [ ] a. A specific adjective replaces a common adjective.
- [ ] b. A specific noun replaces a pronoun.
- [ ] c. A specific verb replaces the verb *be*.

Unity in Paragraphs

UNUSUAL WORK ENVIRONMENTS

CONNECTING TO THE THEME

Read this paragraph about factors for a pleasant working environment. Which do you think were rated most important in a survey? Rank them from 1 (least important) to 4 (most important).

According to a survey of 100 employees, several factors create a pleasant work environment. ___Flexible hours are very important. Many people need to adjust their working day to fit their needs. ___Good lighting can make a work space feel more comfortable. Some workers feel it sets the scene for the work environment. ___A comfortable desk and chair can make working long hours less painful. They can decrease back problems and increase productivity. ___Friendly co-workers are a big plus for almost everyone. People want to like the people they are around for 40 hours a week. These factors and others can help create the best work place experience possible.

survey results from top to bottom: 4, 2, 3, 1

A. Skill Presentation

All paragraphs have a **topic sentence**, several supporting sentences, and a concluding sentence. Supporting sentences are usually specific and give facts or examples to support the topic sentence. These sentences must be directly related to the main idea to give your paragraph **unity** and make it strong and clear. Any sentence not related to the main idea does not belong there.

For example, the paragraph below does not have good unity. The first two supporting sentences are directly related to the main idea in the topic sentence. However, the third supporting sentence does not support the topic sentence. It gives information about a film company, but it does not relate to the idea that some companies work together. This detail does not add to paragraph unity and should not be included.

> [TS]Some film companies work together to make movies. [SS]Disney and Pixar make animated films. [SS]Disney and Pixar sometimes work together. [SS]~~Pixar encourages creative thinking.~~ [CS]Film companies that work together can create more innovative movies.

B. Over to You

1   Check (✓) the paragraph that has better unity.

☐   a.   Innovation is important to the people at Pixar. Pixar uses new technology in their films. The artists at Pixar are encouraged to be creative. Managers want employees to use their imaginations. Most people agree that this company values new ideas.

☐   b.   Innovation is important to the people at Pixar. Pixar uses new technology in their films. The artists at Pixar are encouraged to be creative. Pixar is located in Emeryville, California. Most people agree that this company values new ideas.

2   Read the topic sentence. Check (✓) six supporting sentences that will help give the paragraph unity.

Topic Sentence: Many people believe the clothing company Patagonia offers excellent benefits to employees.

☐   a. Patagonia believes it is important for their employees to be happy and healthy.
☐   b. For instance, many employees take time off to surf, climb mountains, or hike.
☐   c. Hiking is a popular sport in many parts of the United States.
☐   d. Another benefit that Patagonia offers its employees is child care.
☐   e. Employees can bring their children to work.
☐   f. Child care in some cities can be very expensive.
☐   g. Employees are also rewarded for driving hybrid cars.
☐   h. The best parking spots are saved for people who drive those types of cars.
☐   i. Environmentally friendly cars are becoming increasingly popular in the United States.
☐   j. Patagonia is very lucky to have such healthy employees.

CHECK!

1 Supporting sentences should support the _____ sentence of the paragraph.

2 A paragraph that includes only supporting sentences related to the main idea has _____.

C. Practice

1 Read the two topic sentences and each supporting sentence in the chart. Decide which topic sentence each supporting sentence should go with to give the paragraph unity. Check (✓) the box in the correct column.

Topic Sentence 1: Pixar has changed since it started in 1996.

Topic Sentence 2: The work environment at Pixar is unusual.

	TOPIC SENTENCE 1	TOPIC SENTENCE 2
1. By 2010, there were two Pixar offices.		
2. There are brightly colored posters on the walls.		
3. Some employees do not go to the office until the afternoon.		
4. In addition, Pixar is now owned by Disney.		
5. Because of its success, Pixar is now worth more than $7 billion.		
6. Recently, the company started using images of real people in some of its films.		
7. Employees are allowed to play games with their co-workers during the work day.		
8. Sometimes they have contests making paper airplanes.		

2 Match each topic sentence (1–7) with the correct supporting sentence (a–g) that relates to the main idea.

___ **1** Pixar employees have many unusual benefits.

___ **2** Pixar has a creative work environment.

___ **3** Most Pixar employees are satisfied with their jobs.

___ **4** Pixar has had a great deal of success.

___ **5** The company is proud of its diversity.

___ **6** Many animation companies started in California.

___ **7** Pixar has started to use modern technology to create its films.

a For example, they made their first 3D movie in 2009.

b Employees are expected to use their imaginations.

c There are employees from many backgrounds.

d Its films have won more than 200 awards.

e For example, some employees can go to work in the afternoon.

f For example, the Walt Disney Company started near Los Angeles.

g They enjoy going to work every day.

D. Skill Quiz

Check (✓) the correct answer for each item.

1 All sentences in a paragraph
- ☐ a. are general and not specific.
- ☐ b. are related to the same topic.
- ☐ c. introduce new topics.

2 Supporting sentences
- ☐ a. give more information about the main idea.
- ☐ b. are not related to the topic sentence.
- ☐ c. are general and not specific.

3 A paragraph that has unity includes supporting sentences
- ☐ a. that relate only to topics in previous paragraphs.
- ☐ b. that only support the topic sentence.
- ☐ c. that give information about a variety of topics.

4 A piece of writing that has unity is usually
- ☐ a. strong and clear.
- ☐ b. vague and confusing.
- ☐ c. serious and educational.

5 Choose the main idea of this topic sentence: *Some companies believe diversity in the workplace is very important.*
- ☐ a. There are companies that like to have employees with different backgrounds.
- ☐ b. Some employees work better when there are no office distractions.
- ☐ c. Companies with many benefits often have satisfied employees.

6 Choose the main idea of this topic sentence: *Patagonia gives one percent of its profits to charities.*
- ☐ a. Patagonia's profits have grown in the past 40 years.
- ☐ b. Patagonia donates money.
- ☐ c. Groups that help others are important.

7 Choose the supporting sentence for this topic sentence that will not give the paragraph unity: *Some companies believe diversity in the workplace is very important.*
- ☐ a. They believe that employees from different backgrounds make stronger teams.
- ☐ b. To encourage diversity, employers often seek employees from a variety of countries.
- ☐ c. Many companies also provide different resources to their employees.

8 Choose the supporting sentence for this topic sentence that will not give the paragraph unity: *Patagonia gives one percent of its profits to charities.*
- ☐ a. They typically give money to environmental groups.
- ☐ b. Many Patagonia employees enjoy competing in marathons.
- ☐ c. Many Patagonia employees are proud to work for a company that gives money to good causes.

9 Choose the main idea of this topic sentence: *Employees at companies like Pixar and Patagonia are usually satisfied.*
- ☐ a. Some employees want more perks.
- ☐ b. Some employees are distracted.
- ☐ c. Some companies have happy employees.

10 Choose the supporting sentence for this topic sentence that will not give the paragraph unity: *Employees at companies like Pixar and Patagonia are usually satisfied.*
- ☐ a. For example, some of them think they deserve even better benefits.
- ☐ b. These employees have many perks.
- ☐ c. These companies understand how to keep employees happy.

GETTING AN EDUCATION

CONNECTING TO THE THEME

Read these recommendations for paying for school. Which do you follow?

1 Students should try to stay within a weekly or monthly budget.
   A I usually do this. **B** I can't always stay within budget.
   C I don't set budgets.

2 Most schools offer financial aid, such as loans.
   A I have never needed financial aid. **B** I apply for financial aid as needed.
   C I request this each semester.

3 Working part-time can help students pay for college tuition.
   A I work evenings and/or on weekends. **B** I sometimes work during vacations.
   C I don't work.

Mostly As: you are financially independent. Mostly Bs: you could be financially independent with a little effort. Mostly Cs: you are not financially responsible at all.

A. Skill Presentation

There are two main types of writing. **Academic** writing is used for essays, written exams, and e-mails or letters for work or school. It has a more formal tone and is objective, not personal. If opinions are included, they are supported by examples. **Informal** writing is used for notes to friends, personal blogs, and e-mails or letters to friends and family. It has a less formal tone and is often based on personal experience. The writer's opinions are frequently included, often not supported by examples.

One way to make your writing more academic is to use full forms of words. In informal writing, contractions are common. For example, *cannot* is more formal than the contraction *can't*.

Many students ~~can't~~ **cannot** afford college.

A second way to make your writing academic is to use the third person. It makes your writing sound less personal and more objective. Look at these examples. The first is written with a less formal tone. It uses the first and second person, and it includes personal experience. In the second sentence, the third person makes it objective, not personal.

My tuition costs are rising. **You** have to pay a lot of money to go to college.

Tuition costs are rising. **It is** expensive to go to college.

A third way to make your writing academic is to use mostly formal vocabulary. In informal writing, some vocabulary may be informal. For example, *increasing* is more formal than *going up*.

The cost of college is ~~going up~~ **increasing**.

B. Over to You

1 Read the pairs of sentences. Check (✓) the sentence in each pair that is more academic.

1 ☐ a. Many people can't afford to go to college these days.
    ☐ b. Many people cannot afford to go to college these days.

2 ☐ a. You may not know how you'll pay for college.
    ☐ b. Many students do not know how they will pay for college.

3 ☐ a. The college is trying to prevent tuition costs from increasing.
    ☐ b. The college is trying to stop tuition costs from going up.

4 ☐ a. The Curson Academy of Music awards scholarships that cover the entire cost of tuition for particularly talented students.
    ☐ b. The Curson Academy of Music gives a bunch of money that pays all of the tuition for some people.

5 ☐ a. I plan to attend Berea College in Kentucky because I want to participate in their community service program.
    ☐ b. It is required of all students at Berea College to do at least ten hours of community service per week.

2 Read the paragraph. Decide how many and which sentences have an informal tone.

¹Tuition isn't the only expensive thing about college. ²Living on a college campus can be quite expensive. ³Students should set a budget each month for all expenses in addition to tuition and books. ⁴You can get on the Internet free at a lot of colleges, so you probably don't need to worry about that. ⁵However, students should be prepared to spend money on phone bills and possibly on cable television services. ⁶It is important to budget about $200 per month for food, as well. ⁷In addition, purchasing clothing and doing laundry can be expensive. ⁸For example, I spend, like, $50 a month on clothing and laundry. ⁹If you can't walk to your classes, you also need to set aside money for a bus or something like that. ¹⁰Students should plan for a variety of expenses if they are going to live on campus.

_____ sentences have an informal tone. Sentences: _____

CHECK!

1 _____ writing is not personal and uses full forms and the third person. It uses vocabulary that is more formal and specific and has opinions that are supported by examples. We often use this type of writing for essays, written exams, and e-mails or letters for work and for school.

2 _____ writing is often based on personal experiences. It is used for notes to friends, blogs, and e-mails or letters to family and friends and has opinions not always supported by examples.

C. Practice

1 Read each sentence in the chart. Decide if it has a more formal or more informal tone. Check (✓) the box in the correct column.

	MORE FORMAL TONE	MORE INFORMAL TONE
1. You can't afford to buy college books if they're too expensive.		
2. Some students cannot afford to purchase books for college if they are too expensive.		
3. My friends told me their textbooks cost a bunch of money.		
4. The cost of college textbooks can be more than $1,000.		
5. A single college textbook may cost more than $100.		
6. I paid more than $100 for just one book for school.		
7. Some college books are not cheap because they are highly specialized.		
8. Some college books aren't cheap because they are super specialized.		

2 Check (✓) the sentence in each pair that sounds most academic.

1 ☐ a. There are not many scholarship programs at the university.
☐ b. There aren't many scholarship programs at the university.

2 ☐ a. The tuition's increased several times over the years.
☐ b. The tuition has increased several times over the years.

3 ☐ a. I think that grants are a great way to pay for education. They really helped me.
☐ b. Scholarships are a good way to pay for an education because they can cover up to 100 percent of the tuition.

4 ☐ a. The biggest expense many students have in college is books. There are some books that cost more than $100.
☐ b. The biggest expense many students have in college is books. At least the books can be interesting sometimes.

5 ☐ a. I think that getting an athletic scholarship is difficult because it is hard to be good at sports.
☐ b. It can be difficult to obtain an athletic scholarship. Only about two percent of high school athletes receive athletic scholarships.

6 ☐ a. When college students buy used books, they often save money.
☐ b. You can buy used books if you want to save money in college.

7 ☐ a. The academy at York College offers students teaching positions after graduation.
☐ b. There's a college that gives people jobs after they finish school.

8 ☐ a. There are many affordable colleges in the United States.
☐ b. The U.S. definitely has some cheap schools.

D. Skill Quiz

Check (✓) the correct answer for each item.

1 In academic writing, it is important to include
- [ ] a. formal, appropriate vocabulary.
- [ ] b. informal language.
- [ ] c. contractions and slang.

2 Academic writing usually uses
- [ ] a. the first person (*I*, *we*).
- [ ] b. the second person (*you*).
- [ ] c. the third person (*she*, *he*, *it*, or a noun).

3 Which types of texts usually use an academic tone?
- [ ] a. essays and textbooks
- [ ] b. blogs and notes to friends
- [ ] c. e-mails and letters to family

4 Choose the word in this sentence that gives it a more informal tone: *You should have a budget for your expenses.*
- [ ] a. should
- [ ] b. You
- [ ] c. expenses

5 Choose the words in this sentence that give it a more informal tone: *Students aren't going to have enough money if they don't follow their budgets.*
- [ ] a. going, follow
- [ ] b. aren't, don't
- [ ] c. money, budget

6 Choose the word or phrase in this sentence that gives it a more informal tone: *The classes at that college cost a whole lot of money.*
- [ ] a. that college
- [ ] b. cost
- [ ] c. a whole lot of

7 *Colleges are not keeping prices from going up.*
One way to express this idea with a more formal tone is:
- [ ] a. Colleges are not preventing expenses from rising.
- [ ] b. Colleges are not stopping your expenses from rising.
- [ ] c. Colleges aren't stopping expenses from going up.

8 Which sentence has the most academic tone?
- [ ] a. Students often forget that they need money for laundry in college.
- [ ] b. Don't forget that you will probably need money for laundry in college.
- [ ] c. We forgot that we needed cash for laundry in college.

9 Which sentence has the most academic tone?
- [ ] a. The state budget for my college is decreasing annually.
- [ ] b. State budgets for schools are going down every year.
- [ ] c. State budgets for colleges are decreasing annually.

10 Which sentence has the most academic tone?
- [ ] a. Many bookstores do not have used books, so you have to purchase new books.
- [ ] b. Many bookstores don't have used books, so students have to buy new books.
- [ ] c. Many bookstores do not have used books, so students have to purchase new books.

INNOVATIVE MARKETING TECHNIQUES

Coherence

CONNECTING TO THE THEME

How does product placement work?

Product placement is a way companies advertise their products in movies and on TV. No one talks about the product. The product is simply a part of the show. For example, someone on a TV show might be drinking a certain brand of cola. Put these sentences in order to show how product placement can lead to increased sales of the cola.

___ Seeing the product in the store reminds the TV viewers of seeing it on the show.

___ Finally, they buy the cola.

___ First, TV viewers see this brand of cola on the show.

___ Then, they may see the brand of cola while food shopping.

Correct order from top to bottom: 3, 4, 1, 2

A. Skill Presentation

If your writing has **coherence**, it means that it is organized and that your ideas fit together clearly and smoothly. One way to add coherence to your writing is to put your ideas in a clear order, with related ideas near each other. For example, you can put events in time order – the order in which they happen. Look at this paragraph about product placement. The paragraph is coherent. The ideas about computer companies are next to each other, and the ideas about cola are next to each other. The sentences are also in the correct time order.

Product placement is a strategy used for a wide variety of products. Computer companies often use product placement to advertise. Some of them started using product placement in the mid-1980s. Cola companies also have used it since the 1980s. Today, actors may drink **soft drinks** in movies to advertise the product. It is clear that product placement can be an effective strategy for many different **brands**.

Another way to add coherence is to repeat important words. This helps the reader follow the main idea. To avoid too much repetition, use **synonyms** of a word and replace some nouns with pronouns. Read the paragraph again. The writer uses the words *soft drinks* as a way of referring back to *cola* and the word *brand* as a synonym for *product*. The writer used *some of them* to refer to *computer companies*. The writer also used the pronoun *it* to replace *product placement*.

Finally, use transition words and phrases to make your writing more coherent. Transition words and phrases link ideas in your paragraph together. They are usually at the beginning of sentences. You can use a variety of transition words and phrases to link your ideas together, give examples, show time order, or summarize information.

B. Over to You

1 Check (✓) the paragraph that is more coherent.

☐ a. In the 1980s, two movies used product placement successfully to promote candy. In the 1985 movie *The Goonies*, two actors shared a bag of candy. In *E.T.*, the main character ate a certain candy. In 1982, *E.T.* was a popular movie that used product placement. The candy was a part of the story, but it was also advertising the product.

☐ b. In the 1980s, two movies used product placement successfully to promote candy. In 1982, *E.T.* was a popular movie that used product placement. In *E.T.*, the main character ate a certain candy. In the 1985 movie *The Goonies*, two actors shared a bag of candy. The candy was a part of the story, but it was also advertising the product.

2 Read each sentence in the chart. Decide if it is in a clear order or not. Check (✓) the box in the correct column.

	CLEAR	UNCLEAR
1. After that, advertisements appeared in magazines as well. The first advertisements were in newspapers.		
2. The first advertisements were in newspapers. After that, advertisements appeared in magazines as well.		
3. In 1980, $200 million was spent on advertising. Forty years later, $3 billion was spent on advertising.		
4. Forty years later, $3 billion was spent on advertising. In 1980, $200 million was spent on advertising.		
5. Then when you create the ad, use language that appeals to your consumers. Decide who will see your ad before you create it.		
6. Decide who will see your ad before you create it. Then when you create it, use language that appeals to your consumers.		
7. Creative ads can sell a lot of products. Sometimes the most basic ads are the most popular. Creativity also appeals to consumers. Simple ads can appeal to consumers.		

CHECK!

1 To make your writing more coherent, put your _____ in a clear order with related ideas near each other.

2 Repeat important words, but use _____ and _____ to avoid too much repetition.

3 Use _____ words and phrases to help the ideas in your paragraph flow together.

C. Practice

1 Read the paragraph and check (✓) the correct answers.

Advertising in video games is on the rise. More than 100 million adults and teenagers play video games in the United States, and businesses are taking advantage of this. To conclude, advertisers began paying video game companies to include ads for their products. Second, they started to use product placement in certain games. In summary, a video-game character might drink a specific brand of cola or drive a certain kind of car. As a result, video game companies make a lot of money from advertising. For instance, businesses spent $56 million last year on advertisements. For example, experts say that even more money will be spent on marketing in video games in the future.

1 Why do the transition words and phrases in this paragraph make it less coherent?

☐ a. There are too many transition words and phrases.
☐ b. Some transition words and phrases are used incorrectly.

2 Why does the order of sentences in this paragraph help make it more coherent?

☐ a. Sentences with similar ideas are near each other.
☐ b. Sentences about different ideas are added to the end of the paragraph.

3 Important words in this paragraph

☐ a. are repeated, and sometimes synonyms are used.
☐ b. are avoided, and more general words are used instead.

2 Match each sentence (1–7) with a sentence (a–g) from the same paragraph. Look for pronouns and synonyms to help you.

____ 1 Companies consider teenagers' interests when they create new products.

____ 2 Many companies want their employees to be creative.

____ 3 Consumers often react to commercials with positive messages.

____ 4 Advertisements with a negative tone can sometimes be effective.

____ 5 Consumers have various reactions to advertising.

____ 6 Some companies use ads to promote a certain product.

____ 7 Big companies spend millions of dollars in advertising each year.

a Workers who use their imaginations at work are often better at solving problems.

b Negative ads can draw attention to a product and make consumers want to know more about it.

c It may actually become popular if people respond to the ad.

d Teens spend a lot of money on products, and these companies want to appeal to them.

e One business spent over $90 million dollars on commercials.

f An ad with a positive message makes consumers feel good, and it may help to sell products.

g Their immediate response to an ad often makes them decide whether or not to buy it.

D. Skill Quiz

Check (✓) the correct answer for each item.

1 To add coherence to your writing
- ☐ a. use examples, find interesting information, and include facts.
- ☐ b. put ideas in a clear order, repeat important words, and use transition words.
- ☐ c. have a clear main idea, use commas appropriately, and avoid pronouns.

2 What is one way to help make the order of events clear?
- ☐ a. give examples
- ☐ b. repeat important words
- ☐ c. put related ideas together

3 What is one way to repeat ideas but avoid using the same words?
- ☐ a. use pronouns
- ☐ b. use transitions
- ☐ c. use examples

4 Which of the following phrases can be used to add coherence by linking ideas?
- ☐ a. For instance
- ☐ b. By myself
- ☐ c. So what

5 Which sentence shows the use of time order?
- ☐ a. Many large companies advertise on the Internet.
- ☐ b. The Internet is a good place to advertise.
- ☐ c. After that, post your ad on the Internet.

6 To add coherence, which sentence should come after this one?
Companies spend a lot of money on advertisements in video games.
- ☐ a. Advertising became very popular in the 1960s.
- ☐ b. A TV ad during a major event like the Super Bowl can cost millions of dollars.
- ☐ c. They do this because many consumers will see their ads while they play.

7 *Advertisements convince consumers to buy products. Shoppers see ads, and they want to own the products.*
Shoppers and *they* are used to replace which important word?
- ☐ a. consumers
- ☐ b. advertisements
- ☐ c. products

8 Which group of sentences is in a clear order?
- ☐ a. Ads that are well-liked often contribute to higher sales. In other words, products sell better when the ads for them are popular.
- ☐ b. First, buy an online ad that will appeal to consumers. Then decide if you want to buy an ad on the Internet.
- ☐ c. To summarize, people may buy things they see while using the computer. For example, many people see ads on the Internet.

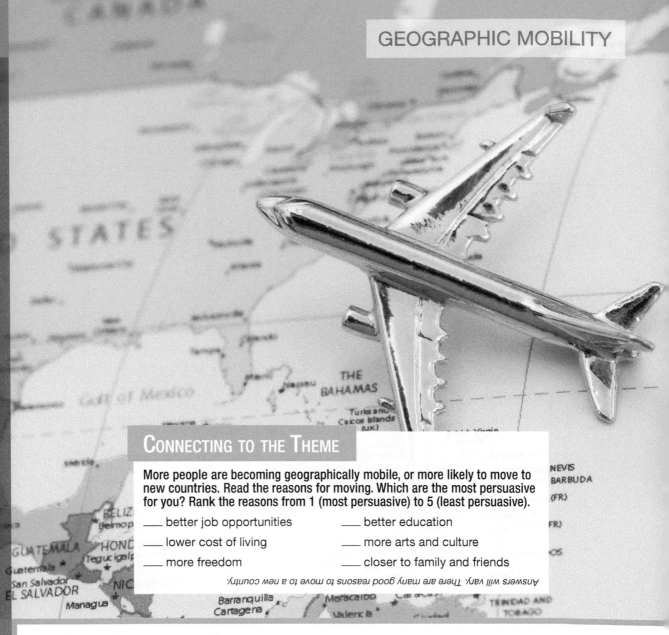

CONNECTING TO THE THEME

More people are becoming geographically mobile, or more likely to move to new countries. Read the reasons for moving. Which are the most persuasive for you? Rank the reasons from 1 (most persuasive) to 5 (least persuasive).

____ better job opportunities   ____ better education

____ lower cost of living   ____ more arts and culture

____ more freedom   ____ closer to family and friends

Answers will vary. There are many good reasons to move to a new country.

A. Skill Presentation

A **descriptive paragraph** describes how something looks, feels, smells, tastes, or sounds. The topic sentence in this paragraph introduces the topic, and the supporting sentences then describe it.

A **comparison paragraph** shows how two things are alike or different. The topic sentence in this paragraph introduces the idea of similarities or differences between two or more things. The supporting sentences then compare them.

A **cause–effect paragraph** explains the causes or effects of an event or the reasons why something happens. It gives the results of something. The topic sentence in this paragraph describes an action or event. The supporting sentences then give the reasons why the action or event happened.

In a **persuasive paragraph**, the writer gives an opinion about a topic and tries to convince readers the opinion is correct or that they should take action. The topic sentence in this paragraph tells the reader what the writer will try to convince them of. The supporting sentences then tell readers why.

B. Over to You

1 **Read each paragraph. Decide what type of paragraph it is and write** *DESCRIPTIVE,*
COMPARISON, CAUSE–EFFECT, **or** *PERSUASIVE.*

1 _____

Korean supermarkets in the United States are similar to supermarkets in South Korea.
Both Korean supermarkets in South Korea and in the United States sell kimchi. Most Korean
supermarkets in South Korea only sell Korean products, but in the United States they
sometimes also sell Japanese products.

2 _____

It is important to support the new Korean supermarket in the neighborhood. The store
offers a variety of products needed in traditional Korean meals. If more people shop at the
market, more Korean products will become available.

3 _____

There are a variety of Korean products in the new supermarket. It is easy to find Korean
products, like spicy kimchi and crisp green Korean pears. The salty smell of fresh fish fills
the aisles.

4 _____

Many Korean immigrants are moving to smaller cities in the United States. They are
moving because smaller towns are more affordable, and there are opportunities to open
small businesses.

2 **Match each sentence (1–6) with the type of paragraph it comes from.**

A Descriptive   **B Cause–effect**   **C Persuasive**   **D Comparison**

____ **1** The bakery was filled with the scent of chocolate and the sound of noisy customers.

____ **2** People who want to learn to speak Spanish should study in Latin America.

____ **3** Chinese speech may sound like singing to someone who is not a native speaker.

____ **4** Cantonese and Mandarin are different dialects, but they share a writing system.

____ **5** Some people find it difficult to learn Chinese because there are so many vowel sounds.

____ **6** It is a good idea for people traveling to China to visit Beijing and Kunming.

CHECK!

1 A _____ paragraph describes how something looks, feels, smells,
tastes, or sounds.

2 In a _____ paragraph, the writer gives an opinion about a topic and
tries to convince readers that the opinion is correct.

3 A _____ paragraph can explain the causes, or reasons, of an event.

4 A _____ paragraph compares two or more things. It shows how
they are alike or how they are different.

C. Practice

1 **Read each sentence in the chart. Decide which type of paragraph it is from. Check (✓) the box in the correct column.**

	DESCRIPTIVE	COMPARISON	CAUSE–EFFECT	PERSUASIVE
1. St. Petersburg is a huge city in Russia. There are many buildings painted blue, yellow, and green.				
2. People should live close to their families. Grandparents should help take care of grandchildren.				
3. Many people relocate more than once in their lifetimes. One reason is that people move to find work.				
4. San Diego and Fairfield are very different. San Diego is a big city, but Fairfield is much smaller.				
5. High-speed Internet is available in big cities, and it is now available in small cities, too.				
6. New products at the Russian market include brightly colored bottles of sweet and tasty soda.				
7. Many offices closed down last year. As a result, many employees moved to new cities.				
8. Relatives should live close to each other. The best option is to live in the same town.				

2 **Read the sentences and write *C* for Comparison, *CE* for Cause–Effect, *D* for Descriptive, or *P* for Persuasive.**

___ **1** Students who study in other countries experience the sights and sounds of another place. For example, they may shop in colorful markets when they have free time.

___ **2** Some students move back home after they study, while other students stay in the new country. Both decisions greatly affect the students' future careers and lifestyles.

___ **3** Many students go to college in other countries. One reason is that they want to learn a new language.

___ **4** Students should study in a country other than their own for a semester. They should experience another culture to learn more about themselves and the world they live in.

D. Skill Quiz

Check (✓) the correct answer for each item.

1. What type of paragraph describes how something looks, feels, smells, tastes, or sounds?
   - ☐ a. a cause–effect paragraph
   - ☐ b. a persuasive paragraph
   - ☐ c. a descriptive paragraph

2. What type of paragraph shows how two subjects are alike or different?
   - ☐ a. a cause–effect paragraph
   - ☐ b. a comparison paragraph
   - ☐ c. a persuasive paragraph

3. What type of paragraph explains reasons or gives results?
   - ☐ a. a cause–effect paragraph
   - ☐ b. a descriptive paragraph
   - ☐ c. a comparison paragraph

4. What type of paragraph tries to convince readers one opinion is the best?
   - ☐ a. a persuasive paragraph
   - ☐ b. a cause–effect paragraph
   - ☐ c. a comparison paragraph

5. *People should eat at the Japanese restaurant downtown.*
   This sentence is most likely from
   - ☐ a. a descriptive paragraph.
   - ☐ b. a cause–effect paragraph.
   - ☐ c. a persuasive paragraph.

6. *The streets in the city are crowded and noisy with people speaking many different languages.*
   This sentence is most likely from
   - ☐ a. a descriptive paragraph.
   - ☐ b. a cause–effect paragraph.
   - ☐ c. a persuasive paragraph.

7. Which sentence is probably from a cause–effect paragraph?
   - ☐ a. The Golden Pig is a Korean restaurant in Cecil, Pennsylvania.
   - ☐ b. It is a good idea to live in a different city after you finish college.
   - ☐ c. Some people move to Cecil, Pennsylvania, because they do not want to live in Pittsburgh anymore.

8. Which sentence is probably from a descriptive paragraph?
   - ☐ a. Austin is a pretty town with a lot of green space and new buildings.
   - ☐ b. You should try some Texas barbecue if you visit Austin.
   - ☐ c. One reason people live in Austin is because there are many things to do.

9. Which sentence is probably from a persuasive paragraph?
   - ☐ a. It is often easier for children to adapt to a new country than it is for adults.
   - ☐ b. Parents should encourage their children to travel to new places.
   - ☐ c. Teenagers often do not like to move because they do not want to leave their friends.

10. Which sentence is probably from a comparison paragraph?
    - ☐ a. It is often easier for children to adapt to a new country than it is for adults.
    - ☐ b. Parents should encourage their children to travel to new places.
    - ☐ c. Teenagers often do not like to move because they do not want to leave their friends.

Descriptive Paragraphs

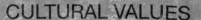

CONNECTING TO THE THEME

During the Industrial Revolution, many Americans lived in villages close to cotton factories. Choose the sentences that describe sounds or smells.

1 The factories were noisy because the machines made very loud sounds.

2 Many workers were needed to run the machines.

3 Workers sometimes sang as they worked.

4 The factories smelled dusty, and workers were exposed to dangerous gases.

5 The workers lived in small, simple houses near the factories.

6 Workers' homes often smelled like the oils from the machines that got on their clothes.

Sentences 1, 3, 4, and 6 describe sounds or smells.

A. Skill Presentation

A **descriptive paragraph** gives your reader a clear picture of a topic. It can describe how something looks, feels, smells, tastes, or sounds. It may be about specific people, places, objects, or events. The first thing to do when you write a descriptive paragraph is to write a **topic sentence**. This gives an overall picture of the topic with the controlling idea. The supporting sentences should help give a paragraph unity. All supporting sentences must relate to the topic sentence and help describe the topic. Look at this example. The topic sentence and supporting sentences all describe the railroad and show how it was impressive. They use details to create a picture in the reader's mind of how the railroad looked, sounded, and smelled.

> ^TS^The railroad was very impressive during the Industrial Revolution. ^SS^The tracks were made of steel and connected many cities. ^SS^The wheels were very large and made loud noises when they rolled on the tracks. ^SS^The trains were powered by burning coal, producing a smoky smell.

A common way to organize a descriptive paragraph is by physical location. This is called spatial organization. For example, you can describe something from bottom to top, from front to back, or from left to right. Look at these supporting sentences from a paragraph about trains during the Industrial Revolution. Notice how the writer used spatial organization, describing the train from front to back.

> The powerful engine was **at the front of** the impressive train. Passengers sat in long cars **in the middle of** the train. There was a person working **at the back** who would stop the noisy train.

(See page 114 for model paragraph.)

B. Over to You

1 **Read the topic sentences and possible supporting sentences. Check (✓) the sentence that relates to the topic sentence and describes the topic.**

1 Sewing machines changed during the Industrial Revolution.

☐ a. The telegraph became popular during the Industrial Revolution.
☐ b. The machines were not very loud, but they made a constant tapping noise.
☐ c. Many people bought the modern sewing machines.

2 Large factories helped drive the Industrial Revolution.

☐ a. They allowed greater production with less cost.
☐ b. They were very smoky and often unclean.
☐ c. The people who worked there were sometimes unhappy.

2 **Number the sentences in the correct spatial order, from bottom to top, to form a paragraph describing settlers' clothing.**

Women wore clothing they made by hand on the wild, unsettled lands of the frontier.

___ They wore warm wool socks in cold weather.

___ On their heads, they wore hats made of soft fabric.

___ They wore long cotton skirts.

___ On top of their socks, they wore shoes made from deerskin.

___ Above the skirts, they usually wore simple blouses.

Frontier clothing was not very stylish, but it was practical.

CHECK!

In a descriptive paragraph:

1 describe how the topic looks, feels, smells, tastes, or _____.

2 give an overall picture of the topic using a _____ sentence.

3 use the _____ sentences to provide the details and describe the topic. Be sure they _____ to the topic sentence.

4 use _____ organization to organize information in your descriptive paragraph. You can describe something from bottom to _____, front to _____, or left to _____.

C. Practice

1 Number the sentences in the correct spatial order, from left to right, to form a paragraph describing settlers' homes.

There is a model of a one-room frontier home at the Museum of the Western Frontier. On the left, there is an iron stove that was used for cooking.

___ There is an open brick fireplace on the right side of the room.

___ There is a large, wooden table with six chairs in the middle of the room.

___ Next to the stove is a small shelf with metal pots and wooden spoons.

People can walk into the model home now and imagine what life was like in the 1800s.

2 Match each topic sentence (1–6) with the correct supporting sentence (a–f).

___ 1 Frontier life was very harsh for new settlers.

___ 2 Today, modern sewing machines have many special features.

___ 3 Many women on the frontier had to cook every meal for their families.

___ 4 The railroad provided a fast way to get from one part of the country to another.

___ 5 People on the frontier wore practical clothing.

___ 6 Homes changed a lot during the Industrial Revolution.

a Often, there was a pot of salty meat stew cooking over the kitchen fire.

b People rode in comfortable passenger cars with wooden seats and dark curtains.

c They often woke up when it was still dark and cold and worked all day under the hot sun.

d Some have small computers inside the base of a plastic machine.

e They wore warm, wool clothing in the winter.

f People started to use electric lighting, which provided brighter light at night.

D. Skill Quiz

Check (✓) the correct answer for each item.

1 What does a descriptive paragraph do?
- ☐ a. It gives reasons why something happened.
- ☐ b. It describes something using details.
- ☐ c. It tries to convince the reader of an opinion.

2 A controlling idea in a descriptive paragraph
- ☐ a. states the topic.
- ☐ b. gives an overall picture of the topic.
- ☐ c. tells the reader to take a specific action.

3 Descriptive paragraphs are commonly organized
- ☐ a. by listing causes first, then effects.
- ☐ b. by comparing two things.
- ☐ c. by spatial organization.

4 Which of the following is an appropriate topic for a descriptive paragraph?
- ☐ a. what a train looks and smells like
- ☐ b. a comparison of different trains
- ☐ c. an opinion that a train is better than a bus

5 Which type of organization would most likely be used in a descriptive paragraph to tell how someone dresses?
- ☐ a. past to present
- ☐ b. cause–effect
- ☐ c. bottom to top

6 Which sentence describes life on the frontier?
- ☐ a. Researchers studied how frontier life changed American values.
- ☐ b. Settlers traveled to the frontier in the nineteenth century.
- ☐ c. Settlers often worked long hours in the hot sun.

7 Which sentence describes how a sewing machine sounds?
- ☐ a. The top of the machine has many silver parts.
- ☐ b. The needle moves up and down rapidly, making a tapping noise.
- ☐ c. The electric sewing machine was a great invention.

8 Which sentence describes the invention of electric lighting?
- ☐ a. Settlers used wood in their cooking stoves and open fireplaces.
- ☐ b. The new invention did not have a bad smell like oil lamps.
- ☐ c. Running water was another great invention.

9 Choose the best supporting sentence for this topic sentence from a descriptive paragraph: *Life during the Industrial Revolution was challenging.*
- ☐ a. Many children worked in crowded factories that were often dusty and dirty.
- ☐ b. Life was easier than it had been on farms.
- ☐ c. Life was also challenging during the Great Depression in the 1930s.

10 Choose the best supporting sentence for this topic sentence from a descriptive paragraph: *James Watt was a Scottish man who helped invent the steam engine.*
- ☐ a. Edinburgh is the capital of Scotland.
- ☐ b. Many other important inventions were developed around the same time.
- ☐ c. He used cold water to produce power for this complicated machine.

Comparison Paragraphs

CONNECTING TO THE THEME

In which ways are printed and electronic books similar? How are they different? Look at the numbered sentences in this paragraph. Which show similarities? Which show differences?

Electronic books, or e-books, and printed books have many similarities. [1]One similarity is that neither e-books nor printed books caught on immediately. [2]Books only became popular after the printing press was invented, and e-books only started to become popular after e-readers were invented. [3]One difference, however, is that people turn printed book pages but simply press a button to move to the next e-reader page. [4]Another is their convenience – you can carry thousands of e-books in one small device! [5]Since the invention of e-readers, e-books are becoming as popular as printed books.

Sentences 1, 2, and 5 show similarities. Sentences 3 and 4 show differences.

A. Skill Presentation

A **comparison paragraph** usually compares two things or ideas, showing how they are alike or different. When you write a **topic sentence** for a comparison paragraph, name the two things that you will compare. Also state how they will be compared, by looking at their similarities, for example. All supporting sentences compare the things or ideas introduced in the topic sentence to give the paragraph unity.

[TS]**E-books** and **printed books** have many similarities. [SS]One similarity is that neither e-books nor printed books caught on immediately. [SS]Another similarity is their appearance.

A common way to organize a comparison paragraph is by using point-by-point organization. First, present one point about both things or ideas, then present another point about both, and so on. Look at this paragraph. Point 1 is about the text size on e-readers and smartphones. Point 2 is about how they are used in different ways.

There are several features that make e-readers and smartphones different. [1]The text on e-readers can be large, **but** the text on smartphones is usually small. [2]**Unlike** smartphones, e-readers are only used for electronic books. Smartphones, **on the other hand**, have many uses. Although they are different, **both** e-readers and smartphones are useful inventions.

You can also use certain words and phrases to help your ideas flow better. Some expressions show similarities, like *similarly, likewise, the same (as), both, also,* and *too*. Other expressions show differences, like *one difference is that, in contrast, however, on the other hand, unlike, whereas,* and *but*.

(See page 114 for model paragraph.)

B. Over to You

1 Read the topic sentence. Check (✓) the sentence that relates to the topic sentence by comparing the two things introduced.

Topic Sentence: Many people find e-books easier to carry than printed books.

☐ a. Not all books are available as e-books.
☐ b. Hardcover books can be very expensive, but sometimes they are on sale.
☐ c. Printed books can be large and heavy, but e-readers are usually small and light.

2 Read the paragraphs and answer the questions. Circle the words and phrases.

1   Many people think that e-books should cost less than print books, but the cost of producing an e-book is about the same as the cost of a print book. Even though e-books do not require paper, other aspects of making e-books cost money. It costs a great deal of money to edit a print book. Likewise, a lot of money is needed to edit an e-book. It does not matter that the format is different because both types of books need to be edited. In addition, it also costs money to promote books. For example, it takes money to create advertisements for a print book. Similarly, it costs money to advertise an e-book. In addition, an author receives money for each print book that is sold. The author also receives money for each e-book that is sold. It may seem cheaper to produce an e-book than a print book, but the costs may actually not be very different.

How many different words and phrases did the writer use to show similarities?
three | five | seven

2   Jack Kilby and Robert Noyce both invented the microchip around the same time. However, they did not invent it together. Kilby was an electrical engineer who worked for a company in Texas. In contrast, Noyce was a scientist who founded two companies in California. Both men went to universities, but Kilby got his Ph.D. in Wisconsin, whereas Noyce got his Ph.D. in Massachusetts. Unlike Noyce, Kilby won a Nobel Prize for his work on the microchip. Noyce lived to be 63 years old. On the other hand, Kilby lived a full life, dying at the age of 82. They may have both had the same idea for an invention, but their biographies are very different.

How many different words and phrases did the writer use to show differences?
four | five | six

CHECK!

1 Comparison paragraphs usually compare two _____ or ideas.

2 They show how these things or ideas are _____ or how they are _____ .

3 When you write a comparison paragraph, state _____ the two things or ideas will be compared.

4 All supporting sentences should _____ the two things or ideas.

5 You can use _____ organization to present one point about both things, then another point about both things, and so on.

C. Practice

1 Read each sentence in the chart. Decide if each one shows a similarity or a difference. Check (✓) the box in the correct column.

	SIMILARITIES	DIFFERENCES
1. People did not think e-readers would be popular. Similarly, they did not believe that microchips would be successful.		
2. Unlike automobiles, bicycles were popular right away.		
3. An e-book may cost as much as a printed book.		
4. Small cell phones are not very expensive anymore, but smartphones can cost a lot of money.		
5. It took years to invent the lightbulb, and it took a long time to invent the telephone, too.		
6. Both Jack Kilby and Robert Noyce helped invent the microchip.		
7. Regular lightbulbs last about 1,000 hours. Energy-efficient lightbulbs, on the other hand, last about 10,000 hours.		
8. Working in an office is often noisy, whereas working at home can be very quiet.		

2 Match each topic sentence (1–6) with the correct supporting sentence (a–f).

___ **1** Televisions and computers share a common history.

___ **2** The invention of the digital camera changed how people take photographs.

___ **3** Watching movies on a computer is very much like watching movies on TV.

___ **4** In my opinion, the new e-readers are much easier to use than older ones.

___ **5** Rockets that go into space and airplanes have some things in common.

___ **6** The museum's exhibits about past and present inventions were educational.

a Film cameras require expensive film. In contrast, digital cameras are much cheaper to use because they do not use film.

b Both inventions fly, and at one time, people thought they would never be possible.

c They had displays explaining the work of inventors from the past. Likewise, they had displays about modern inventors' work.

d It took many years to invent TVs, and it also took years to invent computers.

e TV screens and computer monitors are fairly large, and the picture quality is about the same.

f Unlike the earlier gadgets, the more recent ones can connect to the Internet.

D. Skill Quiz

Check (✓) the correct answer for each item.

1 A cause–effect paragraph may
   - ☐ a. give reasons an event happens.
   - ☐ b. describe how an object looks or what it sounds like.
   - ☐ c. compare two different events.

2 Which of the following is an appropriate topic for a cause–effect paragraph?
   - ☐ a. differences between children and adults
   - ☐ b. the writer's first day of school
   - ☐ c. why children do well in school

3 In a paragraph with a topic sentence about an event's effects, the supporting sentences should
   - ☐ a. show the reasons the event happened.
   - ☐ b. compare the event to another event.
   - ☐ c. show the results of the event.

4 Which of the following words and phrases help show causes (reasons)?
   - ☐ a. as a result, for these reasons
   - ☐ b. due to, one reason is
   - ☐ c. for this reason, consequently

5 Which of the following words and phrases help show effects (results)?
   - ☐ a. another cause is, another reason is
   - ☐ b. one reason is, the most important cause is
   - ☐ c. therefore, consequently

6 Choose the topic sentence that is most appropriate for a cause–effect paragraph.
   - ☐ a. Powerful people often act differently than less powerful people.
   - ☐ b. People can be motivated to save money by a variety of factors.
   - ☐ c. Mr. Paulson was a motivational teacher who was born in the 1960s.

7 Which sentence gives a reason for some people's lack of motivation?
   - ☐ a. People may be unmotivated for several reasons.
   - ☐ b. Consequently, unmotivated people often do not get promoted at work.
   - ☐ c. Some people are unmotivated due to suffering from depression.

8 Which sentence gives a result of a company paying people fair salaries?
   - ☐ a. Therefore, the employees are dedicated to the company.
   - ☐ b. The company pays people more if they work hard.
   - ☐ c. People who are late are not respected.

9 Choose the correct supporting sentence for this topic sentence: *Albert Einstein was motivated by internal rewards.*
   - ☐ a. As a result, he made a lot of money later in life.
   - ☐ b. Due to his desire to find out the secrets of nature, he worked hard.
   - ☐ c. He was born in Germany on March 14, 1879.

10 Choose the correct supporting sentence for this topic sentence: *Albert Einstein had a creative mind and was able to solve many mathematical problems.*
   - ☐ a. Because of this, he came up with theories that changed the world.
   - ☐ b. He rode his bicycle everywhere because he never learned to drive.
   - ☐ c. In addition, he was passionate about music.

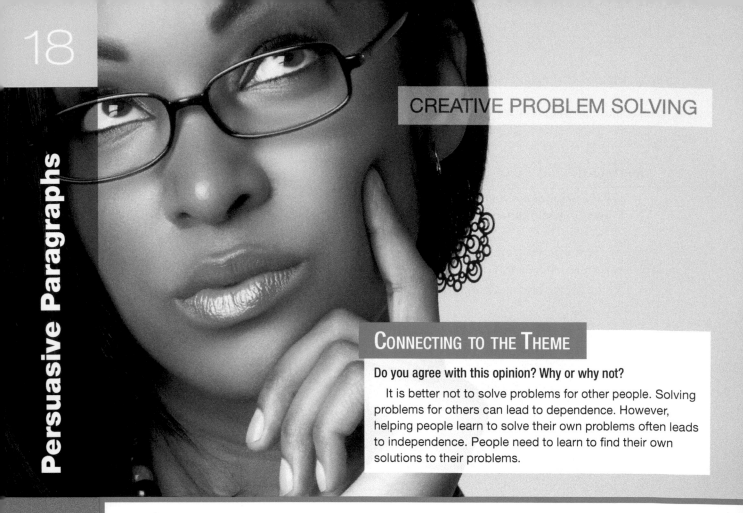

Persuasive Paragraphs

CREATIVE PROBLEM SOLVING

CONNECTING TO THE THEME

Do you agree with this opinion? Why or why not?

It is better not to solve problems for other people. Solving problems for others can lead to dependence. However, helping people learn to solve their own problems often leads to independence. People need to learn to find their own solutions to their problems.

A. Skill Presentation

In a **persuasive paragraph**, the writer gives an opinion about a topic and tries to convince readers the opinion is correct or that they should take action. Write persuasive paragraphs when you have a strong opinion about something and you want others to agree with you. The **topic sentence** for a persuasive paragraph gives your opinion about the topic. Supporting sentences explain your opinion and give facts and examples to support this opinion. All supporting sentences must relate to the topic sentence. Read this paragraph and notice how the supporting sentences explain why it is better not to solve problems for other people.

> [TS]It is better not to solve problems for other people. [SS]Solving problems for others can lead to dependence. [SS]However, helping people learn to solve their own problems often leads to independence. [SS]People need to learn to find their own solutions to their problems.

In persuasive paragraphs, the concluding sentence is extremely important. There are several techniques you can use. [1]First, you can restate the main idea, which is your opinion about the topic. [2]Second, you can offer a suggestion and possibly state an action you want the reader to take. [3]Third, you can make a prediction about the topic that usually supports your opinion. These three concluding sentences are all appropriate for the paragraph above.

> [1]In conclusion, do not solve problems for people without their input.
> [2]For these reasons, you should register for the Help Yourself problem-solving workshop.
> [3]To conclude, if you do not solve problems for others, they may realize that problem-solving is an important skill.

(See page 114 for model paragraph.)

B. Over to You

1 Read the topic sentence from a persuasive paragraph. Check (✓) the sentence that relates to the topic sentence by supporting the opinion that "good communication is important."

Topic Sentence: Good communication is important when solving problems with other people.

☐ a. Expressing ideas openly helps everyone find an acceptable solution.
☐ b. Working with others also helps people get work done faster.
☐ c. Never solve children's problems for them.

2 For the same topic sentence, check (✓) the technique the writer used for each possible concluding sentence.

1 To conclude, people will likely have fewer problems in the future if they communicate with one another well.

☐ a. make a prediction
☐ b. restate the main idea
☐ c. offer a suggestion

2 In summary, good communication is necessary when working out problems with others.

☐ a. make a prediction
☐ b. restate the main idea
☐ c. offer a suggestion

3 For these reasons, communicate with others the next time there is a problem.

☐ a. make a prediction
☐ b. restate the main idea
☐ c. offer a suggestion

CHECK!

1 Write a persuasive paragraph when you want to give your _____ about a topic and try to _____ the reader your opinion is correct.

2 You may also try to convince the reader to take _____.

3 In the _____ sentence of a persuasive paragraph, give your opinion about the topic.

4 Use the _____ sentences to explain your opinion, and remember to include facts and examples to add support.

5 In the _____ sentence, you can restate the main idea, offer a suggestion, or make a prediction about the topic.

C. Practice

1 Read the paragraph and check (✓) the correct answers.

When solving problems in groups at work, it is often effective to involve similar numbers of men and women. One reason for this is that men and women may solve problems differently. In general, women are more likely to look at every angle of a problem. Men, on the other hand, tend to look for quick and practical solutions. Both methods can be effective, so it is often helpful to have men and women coming up with solutions together. Furthermore, an unequal number of men and women may create problems. The gender in the minority may feel uncomfortable. In conclusion, when forming groups to solve problems, companies should try to include about the same number of men and women.

1 What is the topic of the paragraph?

☐ a. the differences between men and women
☐ b. problem solving in groups
☐ c. jobs that appeal to men or women

2 What is the writer's opinion?

☐ a. Problem solving in groups is better with equal numbers of men and women.
☐ b. Women solve problems more effectively than men.
☐ c. Groups should have more men in them because men are more practical and better at problem solving.

3 What suggestion does the writer make for companies?

☐ a. They should get clear advice from men when there is a problem.
☐ b. They should form groups with equal numbers of men and women to solve problems.
☐ c. They should hire exactly as many women as men.

2 Match each topic sentence (1–5) from a persuasive paragraph with the correct concluding sentence (a–e).

____ 1 Brainstorming with others is the best tool for solving problems.

____ 2 It is helpful to be flexible when solving problems.

____ 3 There are many new useful ways to solve problems.

____ 4 Problem-solving workshops are a useful tool to help people learn to solve problems.

____ 5 It is rarely a good idea to solve problems for other people.

a In conclusion, experts suggest trying one of these methods to solve problems in the future.

b For this reason, avoid trying to fix other people's problems.

c People who are willing to try something new will probably have greater success.

d In conclusion, you should discuss many possible solutions when there are problems.

e Register for a problem-solving course in your area to learn these skills.

D. Skill Quiz

Check (✓) the correct answer for each item.

1 Write a persuasive paragraph
  - ☐ a. when you want to explain exactly how something looks or feels.
  - ☐ b. when you want to convince readers of an opinion.
  - ☐ c. when you want to entertain your reader.

2 An appropriate topic for a persuasive paragraph is
  - ☐ a. anything you can describe using time order.
  - ☐ b. something you can compare to something else.
  - ☐ c. something you have a strong opinion about.

3 What is one thing a concluding sentence in a persuasive paragraph can do?
  - ☐ a. It can introduce the main idea.
  - ☐ b. It can suggest an action to take.
  - ☐ c. It can state the opposite opinion of the topic sentence.

4 Choose the most appropriate topic sentence for a persuasive paragraph.
  - ☐ a. Studies suggest that men tend to think of quick solutions to problems.
  - ☐ b. Most researchers agree that children and adults solve problems differently.
  - ☐ c. People should ask for advice when they have a problem.

5 Choose the most appropriate topic sentence for a persuasive paragraph.
  - ☐ a. *Time to Solve* has the most up-to-date information about learning how to solve problems.
  - ☐ b. Buy the book today for help with problem solving.
  - ☐ c. I read *Time to Solve* last week, and then I gave it to my brother.

6 Choose the best supporting sentence for this topic sentence from a persuasive paragraph: *Brainstorming is a highly effective strategy for solving problems.*
  - ☐ a. This is one reason why brainstorming is a waste of time and people should not do it.
  - ☐ b. Brainwriting is a more effective way to think of solutions to problems.
  - ☐ c. It is a useful way to think of multiple solutions to a problem before choosing one.

7 *It is important to discuss problems with others.*
  Which concluding sentence restates the main idea of this topic sentence?
  - ☐ a. In conclusion, some people will try to solve problems without talking to anyone about them.
  - ☐ b. For this reason, you should talk to people about a problem before you choose a solution.
  - ☐ c. For these reasons, discussing problems with others is key.

8 *People should make sure they understand a problem thoroughly before they try to solve it.*
  Which concluding sentence offers a suggestion for an action readers could take?
  - ☐ a. In conclusion, people should make a flow chart to understand a problem before attempting to solve it.
  - ☐ b. In conclusion, computers will help people understand problems better.
  - ☐ c. In conclusion, people should not try to solve problems before they understand the issues.

Using Outside Sources of Information

CONNECTING TO THE THEME

Read these statements about English as a global language. Are they true or false?

1 According to the Business English Index (BEI), a lack of English skills is no longer causing productivity problems (Unknown 2012, www.globalenglish.com).

2 More than 90 percent of companies in Taiwan say their employees need to use English for their jobs (Chang Sheng-eng 2012, www.taipeitimes.com).

3 Almost one million people around the world are currently studying English (Kenneth Beare, date unknown, http://esl.about.com).

1 False (according to the BEI, it is causing problems), 2 True, 3 False (according to one article, more than one billion people are studying English)

A. Skill Presentation

Academic writers often use information from a variety of sources, but it is not possible for readers to ask where these ideas come from. Therefore, in an academic essay, you must include details about where you found ideas. This is called a citation. If you want to include someone else's ideas in your writing, there are two techniques you can use. A **quotation** is when you use another writer's exact words. You must put **quotation marks** around the words.

"International universities attract students with programs taught in English."

You can also show where a quote came from by using an expression like *according to* and the name of the person who said it. Other general expressions include *Research suggests that* and *According to one source*.

The second technique is **paraphrasing**, or putting another writer's idea in your own words by writing the idea in a different way. You must still tell your readers where the idea came from. Below is a paraphrase of the above idea. The writer has used an expression to show that the idea is not his or hers.

According to one source, students look for international universities that offer degrees in English.

Every time you use a quotation or a paraphrase, you must include a citation to tell your reader exactly where you found the information. Give the citation right after a quotation or a paraphrase. If you do not say where the ideas or information came from, it is called plagiarism, which is a very serious offense. At colleges and universities in North America, it is considered stealing. There are a number of acceptable ways to give citations, so ask your teacher which way is correct for your class.

B. Over to You

1 **Read the quotations and paraphrases, and check (✓) the correct answers to the questions.**

1 Which quotation is written correctly?

Quote: We strongly believe that students know the benefits of a degree in English.

- ☐ a. According to one source, "students know the benefits of a degree in English."
- ☐ b. Research suggests that students understand why it is important to learn English.

2 Which paraphrase is correct?

Quote: Some Chinese universities offer an MBA in English, which can help students get better jobs.

- ☐ a. According to Professor Simon, "Some Chinese universities offer an MBA in English."
- ☐ b. According to Professor Simon, there are MBA programs taught in English at some universities in China, which enable attendants to find better professions.

2 **Read the paragraph and answer the questions.**

> ### The Benefits of English Use
>
> A recent article by Dr. Peggy Hobbs argues that the global economy depends on the widespread use of English. The article suggests several specific reasons why knowledge of English is so crucial. According to the article, "The English language is the fourth most commonly spoken native language in the world" (Hobbs 2010, 23). This is one reason why it is often easy for people in different countries to communicate using English. The author further states, "English is the most common second language" (Hobbs 2010, 21). It may be the best way for two people with different native languages to communicate. In addition, Hobbs points out that English is the most common official language in countries around the world (Hobbs 2010, 20). It is likely that some countries use English as their official language because it is important for international communication of all kinds. Finally, according to Hobbs, "English is the language of business and technology, and especially of the Internet" (2010, 23). No matter what your career is, it is likely that knowing English is a useful skill.

1 How many quotations are there in the paragraph? ___

2 How many paraphrases are there in the paragraph? ___

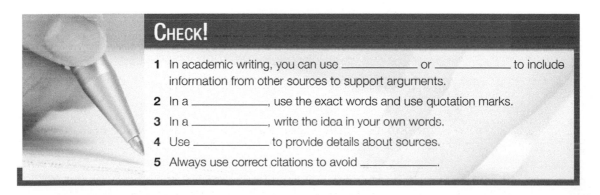

CHECK!

1 In academic writing, you can use _____ or _____ to include information from other sources to support arguments.

2 In a _____, use the exact words and use quotation marks.

3 In a _____, write the idea in your own words.

4 Use _____ to provide details about sources.

5 Always use correct citations to avoid _____.

C. Practice

1   Read the original sentences and check (✓) the correct quotations or paraphrases.

1   English has become an essential language for international careers.

☐   a. The authors of one study wrote that English has become an essential language for international careers.

☐   b. According to one source, "English has become an essential language for international careers."

☐   c. The authors of one study wrote, English is important in international business.

2   Workers in many fields are at a disadvantage if they do not speak English.

☐   a. According to Greta Klaiber, "Workers in many fields are at a disadvantage if they do not speak English."

☐   b. According to Greta Klaiber, workers in many fields are at a disadvantage if they do not speak English.

☐   c. According to Greta Klaiber, "Workers are less prepared if they cannot speak English."

3   English has become the main language for international education.

☐   a. The study states that English has become the main language for international education.

☐   b. The study states, "English is important for international education."

☐   c. The study states, "English has become the main language for international education."

2   Read the original sentences and look at the writer's sentence. Write *Q* if it is a correctly written quotation, *P* if it's a correctly written paraphrase, or *I* if it's written incorrectly.

1   Globalization has increased awareness of other cultures.
____ According to one expert, "Globalization has increased awareness of other cultures."

2   Many young people want to work with people from other countries.
____ A large number of young people want to have co-workers from around the world.

3   Young people find it very exciting to travel to other countries.
____ One researcher suggests, Young people find it very exciting to travel to other countries.

4   English is the official language in many countries.
____ According to one source, some people in China understand a few English words.

5   English is necessary for many international jobs.
____ Studies show that many jobs around the world require English.

6   Many students use English to study business or medicine.
____ One study states, "Many students use English to study business or medicine."

7   Some companies like to know that employees can understand publications written in English.
____ According to one source, most companies will only hire people who can speak English.

D. Skill Quiz

Check (✓) the correct answer for each item.

1. To use a quotation, you must
   - a. express the same idea using different words.
   - b. use a different idea from the author's.
   - c. use the original writer's exact words with quotation marks.

2. To paraphrase, you must
   - a. express the same idea using different words.
   - b. express a different idea using different words.
   - c. use a different idea with quotation marks.

3. A piece of writing that uses someone else's ideas but does not include citations
   - a. is probably considered plagiarism in North America.
   - b. is always acceptable at schools in North America.
   - c. is usually better than writing that does contain citations.

4. Citations give
   - a. general information about where ideas come from.
   - b. additional information that is not in the text.
   - c. specific details about the original source of ideas.

5. Original: *English words can sometimes replace local words.*
   At times, English expressions take the place of local ones.
   This sentence is
   - a. a correctly written quotation.
   - b. a correctly written paraphrase.
   - c. a comma splice.

6. Original: *International business degrees are often more attractive to students.*
   Studies show, International business degrees are often more attractive to students.
   This sentence is
   - a. a correctly written quotation.
   - b. a correctly written paraphrase.
   - c. written incorrectly.

7. Choose the sentence that uses a quotation or paraphrase correctly.
   Original: *English-only graduate schools attract students from many countries.*
   - a. Research shows that English-only graduate schools attract students from many countries.
   - b. According to the author, "English-only graduate schools attract students from many countries."
   - c. One study shows that all schools attract students if they use a variety of languages.

8. Choose the sentence that uses a quotation or paraphrase correctly.
   Original: *The most commonly spoken second language is English.*
   - a. Research shows that more people speak English as a second language than any other language.
   - b. Research shows that "more people speak English as a second language than any other language."
   - c. Research shows that the most commonly spoken second language is English.

FOOD AND SCIENCE

A. Skill Presentation

Depending on your topic and your reason for writing, you may choose to write different types of paragraphs. A **descriptive paragraph** creates a picture for the reader by describing how something looks, feels, smells, tastes, or sounds. It uses adjectives and other details to describe a specific person, place, object, or event. One way to organize a descriptive paragraph is using spatial organization, or organization by physical location.

A **comparison paragraph** compares how two things or ideas are alike and how they are different. It often uses point-by-point organization, in which you present points about both things or ideas, one at a time. Some words and phrases can help show similarities, such as *one similarity is that*, *similarly*, *likewise*, *the same (as)*, *both*, and *also*. Other words and phrases can help show differences, like *one difference is that*, *in contrast*, *however*, *on the other hand*, *unlike*, or *whereas*.

A **cause–effect paragraph** explains the reasons for, or results of, an event or situation. It often uses point-by-point organization. Some words are useful to show reasons: *one reason is*, *another reason is*, *the most important cause is*, *another cause is*, *due to*, and *because of the fact that*. Other words show results, including *as a result*, *for this reason*, *for these reasons*, *consequently*, *because of this*, and *therefore*.

In a **persuasive paragraph**, the writer gives an opinion about a topic and tries to convince the reader the opinion is correct. The concluding sentence in a persuasive paragraph is very important. It can restate the main idea, offer a suggestion, or make a prediction. Writers often use the concluding sentence to suggest that their readers take a specific action.

(See page 114 for model paragraphs.)

B. Over to You

1 **Read the sentences. What is the most appropriate type of paragraph for each one? Write *CE* for Cause–Effect, *C* for Comparison, *D* for Descriptive, or *P* for Persuasive.**

___ **1** Genetically modified rice and genetically modified corn both have features that protect them from insects.

___ **2** Genetically modified foods are tested in large labs with modern equipment.

___ **3** People who do not eat any genetically modified food are healthier and happier.

___ **4** As a result of eating genetically modified foods, certain insects that are important to the environment may die.

2 **Read the paragraph types and topic sentences in the chart. Write the letters of the correct supporting sentences into the correct boxes.**

a This food provides the best way to solve hunger problems throughout the world.

b For example, corn grows well in warm climates, but lettuce grows better in cool climates.

c The bright red tomatoes are extremely juicy, and the corn has a sweet flavor.

d This may have happened because the corn had been genetically modified.

	TOPIC SENTENCES	SUPPORTING SENTENCES
1. Descriptive paragraph	The genetically modified vegetables grown on this farm are fresh and delicious.	
2. Comparison paragraph	Depending on the weather, farmers grow different crops in different parts of the world.	
3. Cause–effect paragraph	In one study, butterflies died after eating one kind of corn.	
4. Persuasive paragraph	People should support the development of genetically modified food.	

CHECK!

1 Use your *topic and your reason for writing | supporting and concluding sentences* to choose a particular paragraph type.

2 Use a *descriptive | comparison* paragraph to describe something.

3 Use a *cause–effect | comparison* paragraph to compare two things or idea.

4 Use a *persuasive | cause–effect* paragraph to show a reason or a result.

5 Use a *persuasive | descriptive* paragraph to convince readers that your opinion is correct.

C. Practice

1 Read the topic sentence from a persuasive paragraph. Then check (✓) three supporting sentences that do not support the topic sentence.

Topic Sentence: Genetically modified corn should not be produced or eaten.

☐ a. Many people agree that the corn does more damage than good.

☐ b. Research shows that the genetically modified corn may harm monarch butterflies.

☐ c. Monarch butterflies have bright orange wings with black stripes.

☐ d. This corn is poisonous to the butterflies, and they sometimes die after eating it.

☐ e. These butterflies typically live for about two months, but bees can live for several years.

☐ f. Research also shows that genetically modified corn may be harmful to humans.

☐ g. For example, some people may have a serious allergic reaction after eating it.

☐ h. Consequently, farmers continue to grow more genetically modified foods.

2 Read all the reasons people want to write about different topics. Check (✓) the most appropriate type of paragraph to use.

	DESCRIPTIVE PARAGRAPH	COMPARISON PARAGRAPH	CAUSE–EFFECT PARAGRAPH	PERSUASIVE PARAGRAPH
1. Tom wants to compare the advantages and disadvantages of new technologies in agriculture.				
2. Sheila wants to write about what genetically modified tomatoes look and taste like.				
3. Jake wants to convince readers to stop buying genetically modified foods in a local grocery store.				
4. Danilo wants to write about the sounds and smells of the food laboratory at her school.				
5. Mia wants to explain some reasons why changing the features of certain foods has led to problems.				
6. Tim wants to convince readers to eat genetically modified rice in order to stay healthy.				
7. Andrea wants to show what wild salmon and genetically modified salmon have in common.				

D. Skill Quiz

Check (✓) the correct answer for each item.

1 A descriptive paragraph often uses
- ☐ a. time order.
- ☐ b. point-by-point organization.
- ☐ c. spatial organization.

2 What is an example of point-by-point organization?
- ☐ a. giving details about an object from top to bottom
- ☐ b. explaining one result, then another result, and so on
- ☐ c. describing events in the order they happen

3 What type of paragraph should a writer use to convince someone to learn more about genetically modified food?
- ☐ a. a cause–effect paragraph
- ☐ b. a persuasive paragraph
- ☐ c. a comparison paragraph

4 What type of paragraph should a writer use to explain the differences between genetically modified rice and regular rice?
- ☐ a. a persuasive paragraph
- ☐ b. a cause–effect paragraph
- ☐ c. a comparison paragraph

5 What type of paragraph should a writer use to show what genetically modified potatoes look and taste like?
- ☐ a. a descriptive paragraph
- ☐ b. a comparison paragraph
- ☐ c. a persuasive paragraph

6 What type of paragraph should a writer use to show the effects genetically modified rice has on children who eat it?
- ☐ a. a descriptive paragraph
- ☐ b. a cause–effect paragraph
- ☐ c. a persuasive paragraph

7 Choose the sentence that is most likely from a cause–effect paragraph.
- ☐ a. Farmers should not be allowed to grow genetically modified food.
- ☐ b. Insects are less likely to destroy genetically modified crops as a result.
- ☐ c. The food science laboratory is clean, white, and very spacious.

8 Choose the sentence that is most likely from a descriptive paragraph.
- ☐ a. Genetically modified rice is the best option for providing healthy food to people living in poverty.
- ☐ b. People should read labels carefully to see whether their food is genetically modified.
- ☐ c. The scientist's voice was clear, and he spoke slowly so everyone could understand his points about genetically modified rice.

9 Choose the sentence that is most likely from a persuasive paragraph.
- ☐ a. The government should give money to people who research genetically modified food.
- ☐ b. The United States spends a large amount of money on food research, and England does, too.
- ☐ c. One reason food research is expensive is because of the fact that the food has to be tested several times.

10 Choose the sentence that is most likely from a comparison paragraph.
- ☐ a. You must read Joan Miller's article on genetically modified rice.
- ☐ b. Genetically modified rice looks slightly different from regular rice.
- ☐ c. Regular rice is white and often grows in large, wet fields.

ALTERNATIVE ENERGY SOURCES

CONNECTING TO THE THEME

Do you agree or disagree with the main points the writer discusses in this paragraph? What information could you add to support your opinion?

These days, many people are concerned about the environment. Some want cars that use alternative fuel sources. Vegetable oil is one fuel source that people are discussing. There are advantages to using vegetable oil instead of gasoline. First, vegetable oil is safer for the environment. It does not release dangerous substances into the air. People argue that this makes vegetable oil better than gasoline. Second, vegetable oil comes from plants. Plants are renewable, meaning farmers can grow more. Gasoline is not renewable. This makes vegetable oil a better long-term solution. Increasing the use of vegetable oil for fuel may help the environment and provide energy to power cars for years to come.

A. Skill Presentation

A paragraph is a group of sentences about one idea. It has a topic sentence, supporting sentences, and a concluding sentence. An **essay** is a piece of writing with several paragraphs about one topic. A common essay format is the five-paragraph essay. In a five-paragraph essay, each paragraph has a special role.

In the **introductory paragraph**, introduce the topic of your essay. Give interesting information to get your reader's attention. Then clearly state the purpose for the essay. This purpose is called a thesis statement. It tells your reader what the essay will be about and often comes at the end of the paragraph. Some thesis statements are more general, and others are more specific. Thesis statements often list the three points that the body paragraphs will discuss. Each body paragraph will give details about one of these points.

The **body paragraphs** of an essay support the thesis statement and give specific ideas and examples. The topic sentences of the body paragraphs tell what each paragraph will be about and they all should relate to the thesis statement.

The **concluding paragraph** of an essay can do several things. It can restate the ideas in your essay by giving a short summary, making a prediction, or making a suggestion.

When you write a five-paragraph essay, remember to include an introductory paragraph with a thesis statement, three body paragraphs that support the thesis, and a concluding paragraph.

(See page 115 for model essay.)

B. Over to You

1 Read the thesis statement and check (✓) the correct topic sentence for a body paragraph from an essay entitled "Alternative Energy Sources."

Thesis Statement: There are many advantages of using electricity instead of gasoline to power cars.

☐ a. There are many kinds of vegetable oil fuel.
☐ b. The environment will be cleaner if people use electric cars.
☐ c. Electricity also powers computers.

2 Look at the different parts of the essay, and circle the correct answer for each item.

Alternative Energy Sources

Some experts claim that we will run out of energy in the future if we do not start using more alternative energy sources. Therefore, people in many countries are currently experimenting with alternative sources of energy. This essay will talk about three natural sources of energy: sun, wind, and waves. —— **1**

Sun, or solar, energy is one example. Large panels convert the heat from the Sun into electricity. This type of energy works well in places where there is a lot of sun, such as in a desert.

Wind energy is another example. Windmills spin faster and faster with high winds. This creates energy. Wind energy is best in places near the ocean or other locations where there is a lot of wind. ———— **3**

Finally, waves are also a source of energy. Special machines in the ocean convert the movement from waves into electricity. Wave energy is possible near oceans, especially oceans where there is a lot of wind.

Depending on their location, people are experimenting with sun, wind, and wave power. They are converting these natural sources to electricity. In the future, everyone should use alternative energy. ———— **5**

2 (bracket around body paragraphs)

1 This part of the essay is a *thesis statement* | *topic sentence* | *conclusion*.

2 These parts of the essay are *the body paragraphs* | *the topic sentences* | *suggestions*.

3 This part of the essay is *a thesis statement* | *a topic sentence* | *a summary*.

4 This part of the essay *introduces the essay* | *gives a new idea* | *restates the main ideas*.

5 This part of the essay *offers a suggestion* | *introduces the topic* | *summarizes the main ideas*.

CHECK!

1 An essay is a piece of writing with several paragraphs about _____ topic.

2 The _____ paragraph introduces the topic and includes the _____ statement.

3 The _____ paragraphs give supporting ideas that relate to the thesis statement.

4 The _____ paragraph can restate the ideas in the essay and make a prediction or a suggestion.

C. Practice

1 Read each sentence in the chart. Decide if it is a thesis statement, a topic sentence, or a concluding sentence. Check (✓) the box in the correct column.

	THESIS STATEMENT	TOPIC SENTENCE	CONCLUDING SENTENCE
1. **From an essay about lowering bills:** You can cut monthly bills by limiting your use of electricity, using less hot water, and making fewer phone calls.			
2. **From an essay about wind energy:** To summarize, it is clear that many countries would benefit by using more wind energy.			
3. **From an essay on how different places are using new forms of energy:** California, for example, tries to increase the use of electric cars.			
4. **From an essay about protecting the environment:** To conclude, going to sleep earlier, recycling plastic bags, and driving less are easy ways to protect the environment.			
5. **From an essay about how businesses can save money:** Businesses can also save money by asking employees to turn off their computers at night.			

2 These paragraphs from an essay entitled "Alternative Energy Sources" are in the wrong order. Choose the correct type of paragraph for each one. Write *I* for Introductory, *B* for Body, or *C* for Concluding.

___ **1** Sun, or solar, energy is one example. Large panels convert the heat from the Sun into energy. This type of energy works well in places where there is a lot of sun, such as in a desert.

___ **2** Finally, waves are also a source of energy. Special machines in the ocean convert the movement from waves into energy. Wave energy is possible near oceans, especially oceans where there is a lot of wind.

___ **3** People are experimenting with various alternative energies. Some alternative energies are better for different locations. Learning about them can help you decide what type of energy is best for your town.

___ **4** Some experts claim that we will run out of energy in the future if we do not start using more alternative energy sources. Therefore, people in many countries are currently experimenting with alternative sources of energy. This essay will talk about three natural sources of energy: sun, wind, and waves.

___ **5** Wind energy is another example. Windmills spin faster and faster with high winds. This creates energy. Wind energy is best in places near the ocean or other locations where there is a lot of wind.

D. Skill Quiz

Check (✓) the correct answer for each item.

1 ___ is a group of sentences about one idea.
- ☐ a. A paragraph
- ☐ b. An essay
- ☐ c. An introduction

2 ___ has several paragraphs about one topic.
- ☐ a. A paragraph
- ☐ b. An essay
- ☐ c. An introduction

3 A thesis statement gives the main idea of
- ☐ a. a paragraph.
- ☐ b. an essay.
- ☐ c. a conclusion.

4 A topic sentence gives the main idea of
- ☐ a. a paragraph.
- ☐ b. an essay.
- ☐ c. a summary.

5 Give interesting information that gets the reader's attention
- ☐ a. in the introduction.
- ☐ b. in the body paragraphs.
- ☐ c. in the conclusion.

6 Choose the sentence that is most likely a topic sentence from a body paragraph of an essay.
- ☐ a. There are three ways people can make a difference by changing everyday habits.
- ☐ b. This essay explains how people can change their habits to make a difference.
- ☐ c. One way people can change their behavior is to cut down on the energy they use at home.

7 Choose the sentence that is most likely the thesis statement of an essay.
- ☐ a. There are several ways people can change their behavior to protect the environment.
- ☐ b. For these reasons, people should change their behavior.
- ☐ c. People can turn off their television when they leave the house.

8 Choose the sentence that is most likely from the concluding paragraph of an essay.
- ☐ a. People save energy by using alternative fuels and by using better light bulbs.
- ☐ b. People must change their behavior, and this essay explained many ways of doing that.
- ☐ c. Some people buy appliances with an EnergyStar label.

9 *As this essay discussed, people are experimenting with alternative energies. Learning about them can help you decide what type of energy is best for your town.* This paragraph
- ☐ a. gives interesting information to get the reader's attention.
- ☐ b. supports the topic by providing details and examples.
- ☐ c. summarizes the ideas in the essay and offers a suggestion.

10 *Ten years ago, people always got free plastic bags in stores. Now this is changing. This shows that people can change their behavior to protect the environment.* This paragraph
- ☐ a. gives interesting information to get the reader's attention.
- ☐ b. supports the topic by providing details and examples.
- ☐ c. summarizes the ideas in the essay and offers a suggestion.

The Introductory Paragraph

CONNECTING TO THE THEME

Which points in this paragraph do you find most interesting? Which points would you like to learn more about?

At a New York clinic, patients don't sign in to see a doctor. Instead, a computer takes a picture of the colored ring in the center of their eyes to identify them. This part of the eye, called the iris, is unique. Therefore, iris recognition is one way to record a person's identity. At the clinic, iris recognition helps keep track of patients without identity documents. Some may have similar names, and doctors want to make sure they treat the right patient. Doctors at the clinic are very happy with the system and can now treat patients accurately and safely.

A. Skill Presentation

When you write an **introductory paragraph**, you need to get the reader's attention and then give general information about the topic. Before you write an introductory paragraph, first choose a topic for your essay. Next, think about the **thesis statement**, or the main point you want to make.

[TS]Using an iris recognition system is an effective way to identify patients.

Then think about the background information the reader needs to know in order to understand the thesis. These will become the supporting sentences that give general background information about the topic.

- [BI]A computer analyzes the iris of an eye.
- [BI]The computer matches a unique iris pattern to an individual.
- [BI]The computer saves the pattern in a database.

Finally, think about why a person should be interested in the topic you're writing about. Some people call this the hook because it should "hook" readers and pull them into your essay.

[HK]Everyone hates filling out paperwork at the doctor's office, but some people can now avoid it because of a new technology.

The hook is usually the first sentence in the introductory paragraph. The background information goes next. Finally, include the thesis statement to tell your reader what the rest of the essay will be about.

[HK]Everyone hates filling out paperwork at the doctor's office, but some people can now avoid it because of a new technology. [BI]With iris recognition technology, a computer analyzes the iris of an eye and matches a unique iris pattern to an individual. [BI]It then saves the pattern in a database. [BI]The next time the person comes to the clinic, she will be properly identified. [TS]There are many reasons why all clinics should use iris recognition for identification.

B. Over to You

1 Read the paragraph and decide what the sentence in bold does. Check (✓) the correct answer.

    Most people do not realize that technology can tell who they are without a passport or even a name. **The science of biometrics uses people's physical characteristics in order to identify them.** It uses information like the distance between the nose and the mouth, the pattern in the iris, or fingerprints. This information is very personal. If it gets into the wrong hands, the results can be terrible. Biometrics can violate personal privacy in several serious ways.

☐   a. It gets the reader's attention.

☐   b. It provides important background information.

☐   c. It gives the overall topic of the essay.

2 The sentences from this introductory paragraph are in the wrong order. Find the hook and label it *H* for Hook. Find three sentences that give background information, and label them *B* for Background. Find the thesis statement and label it *TS* for Thesis Statement.

____ **1** Even if there is a picture or a video of the person who took the child, police have to figure out who that person is.

____ **2** The disappearance of a child is tragic for parents, and finding the criminal who took the child can be nearly impossible for police.

____ **3** There are several reasons why all police departments should have face printing technology.

____ **4** Face printing is one example of a new technology police are using to find these criminals.

____ **5** This new technology can use pictures or videos of the criminal to predict what they will look like in the future.

CHECK!

1 An introductory paragraph is the _____ paragraph of an essay.

2 It usually starts with a _____, which gets the readers' attention.

3 Next, there are several sentences that give _____, or general, information about the topic that readers need to understand.

4 Finally, the _____ _____ tells the reader the topic of the essay, or what the rest of the essay will be about.

C. Practice

1 **Look at the different parts of this introductory paragraph. Circle the correct answers.**

²Your phone knows who you are. ¹New technology helps cell phones recognize their owners. ¹The technology identifies people by their facial features. ¹It allows only the identified owner to use the phone. ¹This technology could prevent problems with stolen devices. ¹It could also stop strangers from reading personal information on phones. ³Cell phone companies should make this technology available for three important reasons.

1 These sentences give *background information | the main topic of the essay | information to get the reader's attention*.

2 This sentence is the *first supporting sentence | thesis statement | hook*.

3 This sentence is the *first supporting sentence | thesis statement | hook*.

2 **Read the introductory paragraphs. They are missing hooks and thesis statements. Check (✓) the correct answers to complete the paragraphs.**

A ___ Recently, scientists began to develop programs that can identify people by their ears. They have developed a new technology called computer vision. Computer vision can identify an ear using a digital picture. However, there can be problems with ear identification. Bad lighting can make the computer think it is seeing a different person. ___

1 What is the best hook for this paragraph?

☐ a. Your ears may soon be used for things other than just listening.
☐ b. Biometrics refers to using data about physical appearance to identify people.
☐ c. The ear consists of three parts: the outer ear, the middle ear, and the inner ear.

2 What is the best thesis statement for this paragraph?

☐ a. Human ears continue to grow throughout a person's life.
☐ b. In addition to this, jewelry can also confuse the technology.
☐ c. Despite some current problems, computer vision will likely become a common way to identify people for a number of reasons.

B ___ That is, a new system allows them to access lunch money using their fingerprints. Parents put money into a special account. They can even tell the system not to let their children buy certain foods. Then, instead of paying with money, the students simply scan their fingerprints. The cost of the meal is taken from their account. ___

3 What is the best hook for this paragraph?

☐ a. Black ink and white paper are often used to take fingerprints.
☐ b. Fingerprinting is sometimes used by police officers who are trying to find a criminal.
☐ c. Thousands of schoolchildren are now getting their lunch by simply using a finger.

4 What is the best thesis statement for this paragraph?

☐ a. Fingerprints are not as reliable as some other technologies like iris identification.
☐ b. Some children buy lunch at the school cafeteria whenever possible, especially when there is pizza.
☐ c. This is a convenient and effective system that can be implemented in any school.

D. Skill Quiz

Check (✓) the correct answer for each item.

1 Which of the following is not found in an introductory paragraph?

☐ a. several specific examples that explain the topic

☐ b. a hook that gets the reader's attention

☐ c. general background information about the topic

2 Which of the following is true of the hook?

☐ a. The hook always gives facts that the reader already knows.

☐ b. The hook is usually the first sentence of the introductory paragraph.

☐ c. The hook is at least two paragraphs long.

3 The thesis statement contains

☐ a. a list of main ideas.

☐ b. the main topic of the essay.

☐ c. information that gets the reader's attention.

4 What is the correct order of information in an introductory paragraph?

☐ a. background information, hook, thesis statement

☐ b. thesis statement, background information, hook

☐ c. hook, background information, thesis statement

5 Which sentence is the most appropriate hook for an essay about new biometric technologies?

☐ a. There are many kinds of biometric technology.

☐ b. Biometric technology is changing life as we know it.

☐ c. Fingerprinting is one kind of technology.

6 Which sentence is the most appropriate hook for an essay about ear recognition?

☐ a. Until recently, identifying people through technologies like ear recognition may have seemed like pure fiction.

☐ b. These advances in technology will improve safety and security for everyone.

☐ c. Computers use databases to organize information about different people.

7 Which sentence is the best thesis statement for an essay about the advantages of biometrics?

☐ a. In the near future, you may be able to pay for things just by using your eyes.

☐ b. These advances in biometric technology may help improve public safety, computer security, and data management.

☐ c. Computers use biometric databases, which are large sets of personal information that are carefully organized.

8 Which sentence is the best thesis statement for an essay about the risks of face printing?

☐ a. DNA tests are a popular way to learn someone's identity.

☐ b. If you have been to an airport or a train station recently, you may have had a "face print."

☐ c. Before face printing becomes widely used, it is important to consider several possible negative effects.

GENERATIONAL DIFFERENCES

Body Paragraphs

CONNECTING TO THE THEME

How are you like Generation Z? How are you different?

Members of Generation X are now in their 40s, and members of Generation Y joined the workforce in the early twenty-first century. Their younger colleagues will be members of Generation Z, people born after the mid-1990s. Most members of Generation Z grew up with technology. They cannot remember a time before the Internet and cell phones. Some researchers think Generation Z workers will be fairly independent. Growing up during a bad economy might also make them more realistic about money. Generation Z workers are likely to be independent, realistic, and comfortable with technology.

A. Skill Presentation

An essay includes a thesis statement in the introductory paragraph. The thesis statement gives the main topic of the essay. Many thesis statements have three main points. In a five-paragraph essay, each point is explained in its own supporting paragraph. The supporting paragraphs are called **body paragraphs**. Each body paragraph begins with a topic sentence. This topic sentence often includes the specific point from the thesis statement.

Supporting sentences follow each body paragraph's topic sentence. They are related to that topic sentence only, not to topic sentences from other body paragraphs. They give specific information about the point from the thesis statement covered in that body paragraph.

> **THESIS STATEMENT:** Members of Generation Z grew up with [1]the Internet, [2]cell phones, and [3]social networking sites.

The three main points in this thesis statement are:

1 Generation Z and the Internet → body paragraph 1
2 Generation Z and cell phones → body paragraph 2
3 Generation Z and social networks → body paragraph 3

The **topic sentence** in the first body paragraph relates to the first point from the thesis statement. The topic sentence and supporting sentences are only about Generation Z and the Internet. The next body paragraph will be about the second point – Generation Z and cell phones – and so on.

> [TS]Members of Generation Z, or Millennials, were raised using the Internet. They cannot remember a time before computers. They have been surfing the Internet since they were young.

B. Over to You

1 Read a second body paragraph from the same essay about Generation Z and technology. Underline the point in the thesis statement that this body paragraph is about.

Cell phones have always been a part of Generation Z's world. They can't imagine life without a mobile phone. They expect to be able to be in touch anywhere, anytime. They are comfortable using the many features of cell phones today.

Thesis Statement: Members of Generation Z grew up with the Internet, cell phones, and social networking sites.

2 Read the thesis statement and the five possible body paragraphs. Check (✓) three body paragraphs that would be appropriate for this essay.

Thesis statement: Millennial employees are confident, have many opinions, and want to succeed.

☐ a. Confidence at work is a trait many Millennials share. They were raised by parents who offered frequent praise. Millennials believed in their abilities as children and carry this confidence into the workplace.

☐ b. Even after age 21, some Millennials still live with their parents. Some people believe Millennials do not want to grow up. Others argue that a poor economy has forced the Millennials to continue living at home.

☐ c. Many Millennials have strong feelings about a variety of topics. They are often eager to share their ideas at work. Even as new employees, Millennials expect their opinions to be heard.

☐ d. Technology is important to Millennials. Some employers allow Millennials to chat and text at work. Others believe that the personal use of technology is a distraction and shouldn't be allowed at work.

☐ e. Many Millennials also desire success. They want to be the best at what they do. Those who are smart, capable, and hardworking should achieve success on the job.

CHECK!

1 A five-paragraph essay often has a thesis statement with _____ main points. There is one _____ paragraph for each point.

2 Body paragraphs begin with a _____ _____ that says what the paragraph will be about.

3 _____ _____ follow each body paragraph's topic sentence and are related only to that topic sentence. They give specific information about the point covered in that body paragraph.

C. Practice

1 **Match the main points of each thesis statement (a–c) with the correct topic sentences (1–3).**

A Thesis Statement: Generation Z employees may be more comfortable with technology, more independent, and more realistic than Generation Y employees.

___ a. more tech savvy   ___ b. more independent   ___ c. more realistic

1 Members of Generation Z will probably want less teamwork than Generation Y.

2 Members of Generation Z have grown up in harder economic times, and they understand they may not get everything they want from a job.

3 Generation Z employees may be better at using technology than Generation Y employees.

B Thesis Statement: Millennial employees are sometimes criticized for being too self-confident, irresponsible, and opinionated.

___ a. too self-confident   ___ b. irresponsible   ___ c. opinionated

1 Millennials sometimes give the impression that they already know everything about the job.

2 Millennials are used to having their ideas heard and are not shy about expressing their thoughts at work.

3 Doing personal tasks online during work can be a serious problem for some Millennials.

2 **Read each thesis statement in the chart and the topic sentences (a–g). Write the three topic sentences that relate to each thesis statement in the correct columns, in the correct order. There is one topic sentence that is unrelated.**

Many Millennials prefer jobs that offer challenges, positive relationships, and freedom of choice.	Many Millennials expect free time, value family, and are active outside of work.
1.	4.
2.	5.
3.	6.

a Playing sports with co-workers is important to many Millennials.

b Many Millennials expect their bosses to listen to their new ideas.

c Many Millennials feel that spending time with their children is very important.

d Most Millennials say they enjoy teamwork and like to build friendships with their colleagues.

e Millennials like to make their own work schedules and choose their own tasks at work.

f Millennials work hard but feel it is important to have a life outside of the office.

g Some Millennials enjoy doing difficult tasks at work.

D. Skill Quiz

Check (✓) the correct answer for each item.

1 A ___ gives the main idea of an essay.
   ☐ a. topic sentence
   ☐ b. thesis statement
   ☐ c. supporting sentence

2 In a five-paragraph essay, many thesis statements have
   ☐ a. three main points.
   ☐ b. five main points.
   ☐ c. two main points.

3 Supporting paragraphs in an essay are called
   ☐ a. topic paragraphs.
   ☐ b. essay paragraphs.
   ☐ c. body paragraphs.

4 Each topic sentence in the body paragraphs should include
   ☐ a. one of the points from the thesis statement.
   ☐ b. all three points from the thesis statement.
   ☐ c. a new point that was not in the thesis statement.

5 Thesis statement: *Millennial workers are sometimes seen as too confident, demanding, and impatient on the job.*
   Which of these topic sentences would not belong in this essay?
   ☐ a. Millennial employees sometimes seem to have too much self-confidence in the workplace.
   ☐ b. Millennial employees often want to move on to a more important job before they are ready.
   ☐ c. Millennial workers prefer to work in teams.

6 Thesis statement: *Young workers expect to have access to social networking sites, cell phones, and the Internet 24 hours a day.*
   In this essay, there would not be a body paragraph about
   ☐ a. young workers' expectations about salary.
   ☐ b. young workers and social networking sites.
   ☐ c. young workers and cell phones.

7 Topic sentence: *Generation Z employees may have to accept jobs with relatively low salaries.*
   Which thesis statement does this topic sentence most likely relate to?
   ☐ a. Generation Z employees may share traits with Generation Y workers, such as confidence, impatience, and outspokenness.
   ☐ b. Generation Z employees may have to lower their expectations about salary, quality of work, and job flexibility.
   ☐ c. Generation Z employees will be self-confident, independent, and driven to succeed at work.

8 Topic sentence: *Millennial workers value making friends with their colleagues.*
   Choose the best supporting sentence for this topic sentence.
   ☐ a. Millennials think that spending time with their families is very important.
   ☐ b. Millennials dislike working long hours and do many activities outside of the workplace.
   ☐ c. Millennials enjoy working on projects with co-workers and going out to dinner with them.

Concluding Paragraphs

MEDIA IN THE UNITED STATES

CONNECTING TO THE THEME

What do you think of the writer's approach to reading news? Would it work for you?

Most people get their news from newspapers and television. As a result, they might hear mostly sad news stories. This could discourage them. However, if they only read good news, they might not know what is going on in the world. One solution is to read both happy news and sad news from many different news sources. Of course, some people may believe that "happy" news is not really news at all, but there are several websites that are proof some people disagree.

A. Skill Presentation

A **concluding paragraph** has several purposes. One purpose is to restate the thesis. Another is to summarize the most important points from the body paragraphs. A final purpose of a concluding paragraph is to give the reader something to think about. Let's look at the thesis statement from the introductory paragraph of an essay about news.

> Some approaches include avoiding negative news, reading positive news, and trying to balance the two.

Several body paragraphs then give more information about the topic and support the thesis statement.

> Some people feel popular news sources focus on tragic and sad news. . . .
> There are a few websites dedicated to reporting only positive news. . . .
> Some experts suggest that you read positive news once a week. . . .

The concluding paragraph then helps remind the reader of the most important points in the essay. The topic sentence often begins with a transition phrase like *To conclude, In summary,* or *In conclusion.* You can then use slightly different words to remind your reader what the essay is about. After that, use supporting sentences to briefly explain the main points of the essay. End your concluding paragraph with a suggestion about what you think people should do, an opinion, or a **prediction**.

> In conclusion, reading a variety of both "happy" and "sad" stories is one way to get more balanced news. Of course, it is important to read about things that are happening in the world. These events may not always be happy. However, finding the right balance of news sources is important to many people. Certain news sources can help you avoid reading only about sad news. [S]Choose the news sources that are best for you. **OR** [O]It is important for everyone to read mostly positive news. **OR** [P]Websites that focus on happy news will probably become very popular in the next ten years.

B. Over to You

1 Read the thesis statement. Underline the sentence in the concluding paragraph that restates the ideas in the thesis using different words. Circle the sentence that offers a suggestion.

Thesis Statement: Balanced news sources include ideas from important leaders, experts, and people in the community.

In summary, balanced news sources represent many points of view. Balanced news stories are important because they help educate the public. The public hears different opinions from a variety of people. This helps them consider other ideas. Read balanced news stories to better understand important events.

2 Read the beginning of each concluding paragraph, and check (✓) the sentence that concludes the paragraph appropriately.

1 Many people choose to read news blogs that reinforce their opinions. They like to read news that reflects their own point of view. ___

- ☐ a. Therefore, people should read blogs about celebrities more often.
- ☐ b. However, it is probably best to read many different types of news blogs.
- ☐ c. Some people prefer blogs that have many colorful pictures.

2 In summary, politicians suggest many different policies. People vote for the policies they believe are best. ___

- ☐ a. People should learn about all the policies before they vote.
- ☐ b. Student elections happen every year in September.
- ☐ c. Many people like to read blogs that reinforce their opinions.

3 More and more people rely on news from a variety of sources. As a result, people are exposed to different ideas. ___

- ☐ a. People who prefer different books will criticize each other more often.
- ☐ b. There are many different places to find news stories these days.
- ☐ c. In the future, there will likely be even more sources for news.

4 In conclusion, some new policies are problematic. These policies are harmful to people in the community. ___

- ☐ a. People in the community deserve better policies.
- ☐ b. Newspapers often report on problematic policies.
- ☐ c. Additionally, people disagree about these policies.

CHECK!

1 A concluding paragraph has _____ purposes.

2 One purpose is to restate the _____ (using slightly different words).

3 A second purpose is to _____ , or briefly explain, the most important points from the body paragraphs.

4 The final purpose is to give readers something to think about. You can offer a _____ , give an _____ , or make a _____ .

C. Practice

1 **Match each thesis statement (1–4) with the correct restatement (a–d).**

___ **1** Relying on news from websites, TV, and magazines helps balance your views.

___ **2** Many people argue that newspapers are the best way to learn about new government policies, current events, and experts' opinions.

___ **3** The news programs people watch often reflect their views about their community, their country, and people in general.

___ **4** Newspapers have exposed some stories that surprised almost everyone.

a Getting the news directly from friends makes it difficult to find out about new ideas.

b Many people choose to watch TV programs that support their opinions about the world.

c Some people believe the best place to find a variety of information is in the newspaper.

d Some news stories have shocked the public.

2 **Number each set of sentences in the correct order to form concluding paragraphs. The restatement of the thesis goes first, then the summary of the main points, and finally a sentence that gives the reader something to think about.**

1 Thesis Statement: Many people dislike news shows that only support one person's opinion.

___ TV news shows should be more balanced and reflect the opinions of a variety of people.
___ In summary, some people criticize TV news shows for sharing only one point of view.
___ Unfortunately, many TV programs reflect the opinion of only one group of people.
___ These people expect news shows to discuss several different perspectives.

2 Thesis Statement: These blogs include only interesting, cheerful, or amusing stories.

___ Blogs that avoid negative news will likely become more popular in the next few years.
___ To conclude, many blogs include only positive stories.
___ Other blogs share "happy" news from different parts of the world.
___ Some blogs have stories about people who were heroes.

3 Thesis Statement: Most people have access to the Internet and several TV news shows.

___ Some people read just one online news site. Other people only watch TV news.
___ Finally, a few people read several online news sites and watch TV news shows.
___ People should get their news from all of these sources.
___ In summary, people can usually choose where to get their news.

4 Thesis Statement: People who write newspaper articles often reveal surprising facts about different issues.

___ For instance, these newspaper reporters might help people better understand a complicated environmental problem.
___ Newspaper reporters can help educate the public about a variety of problems.
___ Newspapers should be responsible for exposing stories and educating the public.
___ In conclusion, newspapers often expose issues the public does not know about.

D. Skill Quiz

Check (✓) the correct answer for each item.

1 In the concluding paragraph of an essay, the thesis statement should be
   - ☐ a. repeated using different words.
   - ☐ b. repeated using the same words.
   - ☐ c. added to the end of the paragraph.

2 Which transition phrase can begin the topic sentence of a concluding paragraph?
   - ☐ a. One reason is
   - ☐ b. In contrast
   - ☐ c. In summary

3 The concluding paragraph of an essay
   - ☐ a. reminds the reader about one point from the thesis statement.
   - ☐ b. summarizes information from the body paragraphs.
   - ☐ c. includes a hook with information to get the reader's attention.

4 A concluding paragraph should
   - ☐ a. give the reader something to think about.
   - ☐ b. follow the introductory paragraph.
   - ☐ c. support only one point from the thesis statement.

5 A concluding paragraph can end with
   - ☐ a. an unrelated idea.
   - ☐ b. a thesis statement.
   - ☐ c. a suggestion.

6 Choose the sentence that restates this thesis statement: *Anyone can read local newspapers, political blogs, and websites to find out more about certain policies.*
   - ☐ a. In my opinion, newspapers are the best way to get the news.
   - ☐ b. In summary, people can use a variety of resources to learn more about these policies.
   - ☐ c. On the other hand, blogs are becoming increasingly popular.

7 Choose the sentence that restates this thesis statement: *Some politicians are not well-liked because their policies are unclear, not useful, or ineffective.*
   - ☐ a. In the future, politicians will make policies that protect children.
   - ☐ b. For example, some politicians create policies that people do not like.
   - ☐ c. In conclusion, politicians who do not create clear, useful, and effective policies are often unpopular.

8 Choose the concluding sentence that makes a prediction.
   - ☐ a. People should listen to news on Internet radio stations.
   - ☐ b. Listening to news from the radio is the best way to get information.
   - ☐ c. Radio news will likely become more popular in the future.

9 Choose the concluding sentence that offers a suggestion.
   - ☐ a. Newspaper writers should expose important issues.
   - ☐ b. Reading newspaper articles about important issues is enjoyable.
   - ☐ c. Newspapers will continue to expose important issues in the future.

10 Choose the concluding sentence that gives an opinion.
   - ☐ a. News programs on TV will continue to report mostly bad news.
   - ☐ b. It is relaxing to watch news programs on TV.
   - ☐ c. News programs on TV are common.

Descriptive Essays

NATURAL DISASTERS

CONNECTING TO THE THEME

Underline the details that you remember from the 2010 eruption. What other details do you know of?

The 2010 eruption of a volcano called "E15" affected almost every country in Europe. The volcano erupted in Iceland on April 14. Fire and hot rocks exploded from the top but did not cause much damage. On the other hand, ice and ash from the volcano caused major problems. Ice melted and made rivers rise, causing 800 people to leave their homes. Experts feared that the ash would hurt airplane engines. As a result, many European airports closed for more than a week. In conclusion, the eruption of E15 was devastating to people throughout Europe.

A. Skill Presentation

A **descriptive essay** gives a detailed picture of a topic. It describes how something looks, feels, smells, tastes, or sounds. Like all essays, a descriptive essay has an introductory paragraph, body paragraphs, and a concluding paragraph.

In the introductory paragraph, give a basic description of your topic and general background information. Try to get the reader interested in your topic. The thesis statement should be the last sentence. In the thesis statement, state the main idea of the essay and what you will describe.

Each body paragraph should describe a different aspect of the topic you gave in the thesis statement by giving details about how things look, smell, feel, taste, or sound. Remember, each body paragraph should have a topic sentence that relates to the main idea in the thesis statement and that tells the aspect of the essay topic it will describe.

In the concluding paragraph, summarize the main points from the body paragraphs and remind the reader of the most important details and descriptions. It should leave the reader with an overall impression of the essay topic.

When you write a descriptive essay, organize your ideas clearly. To do this, you can use spatial organization. For example, describe something from bottom to top, front to back, or left to right. This works best if you are describing a specific place or a specific object. Another common way to organize a descriptive essay is time order, in which you organize events in the order they happened. Choose the type of organization that works best for your topic.

(See page 116 for model essay.)

B. Over to You

Read the essay excerpt and check (✓) the correct answers.

On January 12, 2010, an earthquake devastated Haiti. Thousands of people died, but at least one story had a positive outcome. Darlene Etienne was trapped under her home for 15 days. However, she was rescued and miraculously recovered.

Darlene was trapped for more than two weeks under what used to be her home. She could not move, and she did not have anything to eat or drink.

Darlene was rescued after a neighbor heard her voice. He and others began to dig, and soon French rescue workers arrived. Gradually, they opened a hole, and they pulled her out. . . .

Darlene survived the earthquake and eventually recovered. She was immediately taken to a hospital and treated by capable doctors. . . .

In conclusion, Darlene's rescue was a bright spot during a tragic time. After being trapped for two weeks, she was saved by rescue workers. She was treated in a hospital and is doing well.

1 What is the thesis statement of this essay?

    ☐ a. On January 12, 2010, an earthquake devastated Haiti.

    ☐ b. Darlene Etienne was trapped under her home for 15 days. However, she was rescued and miraculously recovered.

    ☐ c. Her story gave many people hope during a major catastrophe.

2 The first body paragraph describes

    ☐ a. being trapped.

    ☐ b. the people who Darlene met in the hospital.

    ☐ c. what Darlene did before she was trapped.

3 The second body paragraph describes

    ☐ a. Darlene's neighbor and his family.

    ☐ b. what tools the rescue workers used.

    ☐ c. how Darlene was rescued.

4 The third body paragraph describes

    ☐ a. Darlene's family.

    ☐ b. Darlene's recovery.

    ☐ c. what the hospital looked like.

5 The essay is organized using

    ☐ a. spatial organization.

    ☐ b. time order.

    ☐ c. point-by-point organization.

CHECK!

1 The _____ paragraph of a descriptive essay gives a basic description of the topic and general background information.

2 The _____ paragraphs include details about how things look, smell, feel, taste, or sound.

3 The _____ paragraph summarizes the main points of the essay.

C. Practice

1 Read the thesis statement from a descriptive essay. Match the supporting sentences (a–c) from each body paragraph to the correct topic sentences (1–3).

Thesis Statement: Many earthquakes caused catastrophes in 2010 around the world.

___ **1** The January 12 earthquake in Haiti was one of the most devastating natural disasters in history.

___ **2** The earthquake in Chile on February 27 was another event that devastated many people.

___ **3** A third terrible disaster was the earthquake in China that happened in April.

a It was so strong that some people felt it in Argentina. Homes, hospitals, and other buildings were destroyed, leaving large piles of rock and cement in many areas.

b This earthquake hit the center of the country, about 1,500 miles from Beijing. Many homes were destroyed. Rescue workers gave people warm coats and tents.

c More than 200,000 people died, and more than one million Haitians were homeless after the quake. Cities were noisy and frightening as people tried to rescue others.

2 Read the thesis statement and number the paragraph excerpts to put them in the correct time order from the first event to the last event.

Thesis statement: Rescue workers from Los Angeles were well prepared to help earthquake victims in Haiti.

___ The fire department then gathered a team of medical experts and rescuers. Members of the team had trained for years to deal with devastating events like this. They learned how to find victims trapped under heavy rocks or fallen buildings. . . .

___ In conclusion, teams organized by the fire department had been specially trained to help in disasters. They had to make many preparations before they could go to Haiti. . . .

___ First, the U.S. government asked the Los Angeles County Fire Department to help. They asked the fire department to put together an experienced team to help the victims in Haiti. . . .

___ The team gathered special equipment right before they left on their trip. In addition to heavy equipment for moving large objects, they also took rescue dogs. . . .

3 Read the thesis statement and number the paragraph excerpts in the correct spatial order from front to back.

Thesis Statement: Rescue worker Jill Meadows was shocked when she entered the chaotic emergency center.

___ When Jill Meadows arrived at the medical center, she was surprised to see a hectic environment. To summarize, the center was one large room with three different areas. The reception area was at the front. . . .

___ At the back of the room, doctors were helping the patients with the most serious problems first. The area was divided into six small rooms separated by temporary plastic walls. . . .

___ In the middle of the room, Meadows noticed many wounded patients were waiting on the floor. Some were sitting on blankets, and many people were holding small children. . . .

___ When she arrived at the center, the front of the room was already busy and filled with people. It was a temporary reception area for people who needed help to check in. . . .

D. Skill Quiz

Check (✓) the correct answer for each item.

1 A descriptive essay

  ☐ a. gives the reasons something happens.

  ☐ b. creates a picture of person, place, object, or event.

  ☐ c. states an opinion about a topic.

2 The thesis statement of a descriptive essay

  ☐ a. gives background information about the topic.

  ☐ b. states the main idea of the essay.

  ☐ c. gets the reader interested in the topic.

3 The body paragraphs of a descriptive essay

  ☐ a. get the reader interested in the topic.

  ☐ b. summarize the main points.

  ☐ c. describe different aspects of the overall topic of the essay.

4 What would be the best way to organize an essay describing events in a rescue worker's life?

  ☐ a. spatial order from top to bottom

  ☐ b. spatial order from left to right

  ☐ c. time order

5 Choose the most appropriate thesis statement for an essay describing Hurricane Katrina.

  ☐ a. Hurricane Katrina drastically changed the lives of children and adults in New Orleans.

  ☐ b. There were many hurricanes in the United States in 2005.

  ☐ c. Hurricane Cindy was not as devastating as Hurricane Katrina.

6 Choose the most appropriate thesis statement for an essay describing an organization that helps people.

  ☐ a. Oxfam started in 1942, but Oxfam America did not start until 1970.

  ☐ b. Everyone should give money to Oxfam to help people.

  ☐ c. Oxfam has education programs, programs that help people in poverty-stricken areas, and emergency assistance programs.

7 Choose the most appropriate topic sentence for a body paragraph in an essay describing the earthquake in Haiti.

  ☐ a. In conclusion, the earthquake in Haiti was one of the worst catastrophes in 2010.

  ☐ b. There were several major earthquakes that year, including one in Haiti, one in Chile, and one in China.

  ☐ c. Areas of the capital city were completely destroyed because many buildings fell.

8 Choose the most appropriate sentence from a concluding paragraph for an essay with this thesis statement: *Oxfam America helps people around the world.*

  ☐ a. In summary, many people benefit from Oxfam America's global programs.

  ☐ b. To conclude, the Red Cross is another organization that helps people.

  ☐ c. To summarize, Oxfam America started in 1970.

26

CONNECTING TO THE THEME

Which do you prefer, Tex-Mex or traditional Mexican food? Why do you think Tex-Mex foods gradually changed?

Mexican foods and Texan "Tex-Mex" foods are similar in many ways and different in others. People usually have chips and salsa before a Tex-Mex dinner. Salsa is popular in Mexico, but people do not usually eat it with chips. There are also differences in the ingredients. For instance, many Tex-Mex dishes include yellow or orange cheese. Cheese is not as common in Mexican dishes, which usually use a soft white cheese. In addition, dishes commonly found in Mexico can be difficult to get in the United States. On the other hand, common Tex-Mex desserts may not be available in Mexico. Although Mexican foods influenced Mexican-American foods, there are many differences between the two.

A. Skill Presentation

A **comparison essay** compares two or more things, such as two kinds of foods or two types of restaurants. It shows how they are alike or how they are different. Like all essays, a comparison essay has an introductory paragraph, body paragraphs, and a concluding paragraph.

In the introductory paragraph of a comparison essay, give general background information and get the reader interested in your topic. Clearly state the two things you are going to compare in the thesis statement. The thesis statement is the last sentence of the introductory paragraph. It says what the rest of the essay will be about.

In the body paragraphs of a comparison essay, compare different aspects of the topic. Each topic sentence relates directly to the topic in the thesis statement. Each topic sentence tells what aspect of the main idea will be compared in that paragraph.

In the concluding paragraph of a comparison essay, restate the thesis statement and summarize the main points of the essay. You can also give your opinion, offer a suggestion, or make a prediction about the topic. The first sentence restates the main idea of the essay. The second and third sentences summarize the main points of the essay.

(See page 117 for model essay.)

B. Over to You

1 **Read the comparison essay excerpt and check (✓) the correct answers.**

Chinese food is popular worldwide. It has become very popular in the U.S. Some Chinese restaurants in the U.S. serve food that is also served in China, but many adapt food to appeal to Americans. ___
The way Chinese food is cooked in the U.S is often different from how it is cooked in China. . . .
Chinese food in China has more variety than it does in the U.S. . . .
Some Chinese-American foods are not originally from China. . . .
In conclusion, there are some major differences between Chinese and Chinese-American food. The way the food is cooked can be different. Chinese food has more variety than Chinese-American food, and some Chinese-American foods are not found in China. ___

1 What's the best thesis statement for the essay?

    a. There are three key differences between traditional Chinese food and Chinese-style food served in American restaurants.

    b. Aside from Chinese foods, many Americans also enjoy a variety of Japanese foods.

    c. Americans and Chinese people have identical preferences when it comes to food.

2 What's the most appropriate concluding sentence for the essay?

    a. Chinese people should learn how to use American ingredients in their cooking.

    b. Even as Chinese people continue to move to the U.S., it is likely that Chinese-American food will remain quite different from traditional Chinese food.

    c. Chinese restaurants are the best place for Americans to learn about Chinese culture.

2 **Read the thesis statement and number the paragraph excerpts in the most logical order.**

Thesis Statement: Jajangmyeon and tangsuyuk are "Chinese" dishes that are popular in Korea but different from traditional dishes in China.

___ Tangsuyuk is another Korean-Chinese dish. It has pork, onions, peppers, and pineapples. This dish is also popular in Chinese restaurants in the U.S., but it is not a traditional dish in China. . . .

___ Jajangmyeon is based on a Chinese dish. The Korean-Chinese dish is different because the sauce contains a paste made from black soybeans, which are not used in the Chinese dish. . . .

___ In conclusion, many people in South Korea eat "Chinese" food that is different from real Chinese food in China. Jajangmyeon and tangsuyuk are three popular Korean-Chinese dishes that differ from traditional Chinese dishes. . . .

CHECK!

1 A comparison essay compares _____ or more things.

2 The introductory paragraph of a comparison essay gives general _____ information and gets the reader interested in your topic.

3 The thesis statement clearly _____ what you are going to compare.

4 The body paragraphs compare different _____ of the essay topic.

5 The concluding paragraph _____ the thesis statement and _____ the main points of the essay.

C. Practice

1 Read the excerpt from a comparison essay, and check (✓) the correct answers.

International food is becoming popular in the U.S. For example, there are Mexican, Italian, and Chinese restaurants almost everywhere in the U.S. Some are privately owned restaurants. Others are large chain restaurants. American restaurants that serve international foods have key differences depending on whether they are local or part of a chain.

Small, local restaurants offer many special dishes that bigger chain restaurants do not offer. For example, a small Tex-Mex restaurant may offer fresh tortilla soup. . . .

Also, people with a close connection to a certain country may be more likely to own a small local restaurant than a chain restaurant. For this reason, . . .

To conclude, small local restaurants and large chain restaurants with international food have several important differences. Local restaurants often serve special dishes with authentic ingredients. Chain restaurants sometimes serve food that is less authentic but easier to prepare. Finally, some people argue that local restaurants may also have a more authentic atmosphere. To experience traditional food from other countries, it is usually better to try a local restaurant first.

1 What is the thesis statement?

☐ a. International food is becoming popular in the U.S.

☐ b. To conclude, small local restaurants and large chain restaurants with international food have several important differences.

☐ c. American restaurants that serve international foods have key differences depending on whether they are local or part of a chain.

2 The comparison made in the essay shows

☐ a. how two aspects of the topic are alike.

☐ b. how two aspects of the topic are different.

☐ c. how two aspects of the topic are alike and how they are different.

3 What does the last sentence of the concluding paragraph do?

☐ a. summarizes the essay

☐ b. offers a suggestion

☐ c. makes a prediction

2 Read the thesis statement for a comparison essay. Match each supporting sentence (a–c) with the correct topic sentence (1–3).

Thesis Statement: Many U.S.-based fast-food chain restaurants adapt their menus in different countries around the world.

____ **1** Fast-food chain restaurants in certain countries often use ingredients other than meat.

____ **2** Many fast-food chains based in the United States use different toppings for their burgers in other countries.

____ **3** U.S.-based chain restaurants also change their drinks in other countries.

a In Korea, kimchi is used on hamburgers in chain restaurants. Teriyaki sauce is used to flavor some burgers in chain restaurants in Japan.

b In India, some restaurants serve vegetarian hamburgers. In Japan, some pizza chains put squid on their pizza instead of meat.

c In some countries, restaurants serve local sodas that are not as sweet as American sodas.

D. Skill Quiz

Check (✓) the correct answer for each item.

1 What does a comparison essay do?
  - ☐ a. It explains how two things are alike or different.
  - ☐ b. It gives a picture of a specific person, place, object, or event.
  - ☐ c. It shows the reasons why something happens.

2 What is the purpose of the thesis statement in a comparison essay?
  - ☐ a. to provide general background information about the topic
  - ☐ b. to give the main idea of the essay
  - ☐ c. to get the reader's attention

3 What can a concluding paragraph of a comparison essay do?
  - ☐ a. get the reader interested in the topic
  - ☐ b. make a prediction about the topic
  - ☐ c. explain new ways that aspects of the topic are different

4 Choose the best thesis statement for an essay comparing Indian food in India and in North America.
  - ☐ a. There are many authentic Indian restaurants in New York.
  - ☐ b. Indian food in North America is similar to Indian food in India.
  - ☐ c. Indian food is popular worldwide, especially in the United Kingdom.

5 Choose the best thesis statement for an essay comparing Tex-Mex food and New Mexican food.
  - ☐ a. New Mexican food typically uses a lot of red chilis.
  - ☐ b. A fish taco is an excellent example of Tex-Mex food.
  - ☐ c. Tex-Mex food comes from Texas, whereas New Mexican food is traditionally found in New Mexico.

6 Choose the best topic sentence for a body paragraph in an essay comparing cooking Chinese food at home and in restaurants in the U.S.
  - ☐ a. Some people do not cook Chinese food at home because their stoves are not as hot as restaurant stoves.
  - ☐ b. Many people get food at take-out Chinese restaurants instead of eating at the restaurant.
  - ☐ c. Many Chinese Americans cook Chinese food at home, although they prepare dishes from different areas of the country.

7 Choose the sentence from the concluding paragraph of an essay with this thesis statement: *Food in Thai restaurants in the U.S. is similar to food in Thailand.*
  - ☐ a. In summary, many people in the U.S. use a fork to eat Thai food.
  - ☐ b. To conclude, there are not many differences between American-style Thai food and food in Thailand.
  - ☐ c. To summarize, the best place to get Thai food in the U.S. is Chicago.

8 Choose the sentence from the concluding paragraph of an essay with this thesis statement: *In the United States, Chinese buffet restaurants often serve dishes that are different from those in Chinese take-out restaurants.*
  - ☐ a. As Americans try more kinds of Chinese food, they will eat more of the foods in Chinese buffets.
  - ☐ b. People pay one price for foods at a buffet, but they pay for each dish at a take-out restaurant.
  - ☐ c. Buffets are a good choice for travelers on a budget.

The Steps of Essay Writing

CONSUMERISM

CONNECTING TO THE THEME

Have you or someone you know ever been a victim of "lifestyle creep"? What kinds of things did you buy?

Sometimes, things that start out as "extras" can begin to feel like necessities. This process has been called "lifestyle creep." For example, a family might wash their clothes at a laundromat for years. Then they move into a house that has a washing machine and a dryer. The next time they move, they look for a house with these appliances because they now feel they are necessary. Another example of lifestyle creep is a man of modest income who buys expensive suits only for special occasions. Later, he starts to want more and more expensive items. People who continue to buy new things when they do not need them may be victims of "lifestyle creep."

A. Skill Presentation

When you write an essay, you should follow several steps to make sure your writing is clear and interesting. Some steps are part of the prewriting process. Follow these steps before writing:

1 **Choose an appropriate topic.** For example, maybe you would like to write an essay about shopping addicts. Write down a few reasons why you want to write about this topic. This step will help you narrow your ideas.

2 **Make a list of ideas.** Research your topic and write down everything related to the topic that you can think of. In this step, use words and phrases, not complete sentences. This will save time.

3 **Make an outline.** You can use ideas from a list to make your outline, but you'll need to include more details. An outline often includes the thesis statement for the essay and shows specifically what each paragraph will be about. Outlines help writers organize their thoughts and make sure their essays have a logical flow.

Once you have finished the prewriting steps, you are ready to write and revise your essay. Write a first draft using the outline you have made. Then go back and read the draft several times. Make sure your ideas are clear. Next, revise your essay. Add more details, facts, or examples to help explain things that are not clear. Remove extra details that are not necessary.

The final step of the essay-writing process is to edit your essay and write a final draft. When you edit, correct grammar mistakes and spelling mistakes. Once you have finished editing your essay, show it to a teacher, friend, or family member. Ask them to edit it, too. After you have finished editing, write your final draft. This is the draft that you will hand in to your teacher.

B. Over to You

1 **Write the correct prewriting steps to label the texts.**

Outline your essay   **Choose a topic**   **Make a list of ideas**

1 _____

Online shopping behavior
• I have noticed that more and more people are shopping online.
• I wonder if people behave differently when they shop online instead of in a store.

2 _____

What people look for when shopping online:
• making purchases quickly
• reviews from other shoppers
• lower prices than in store

3 _____

Thesis statement: Some experts say that people behave differently when they shop online than when they shop in stores.
Body paragraph 1: shopping online is often faster
Body paragraph 2: prices are lower online
Body paragraph 3: shoppers can see other people's opinions online
Conclusion: In the future, more people will shop online because it is faster, cheaper, and more interactive than shopping in a store.

2 **Match each list of ideas (1–3) with the correct essay topic (a–c).**

___ **1** • clothing a person doesn't need
    • food from restaurants

___ **2** • many credit cards
    • hiding purchases from family

___ **3** • compare prices
    • do not overspend

a Making a big purchase

b Unnecessary expenses

c Signs of a shopping addiction

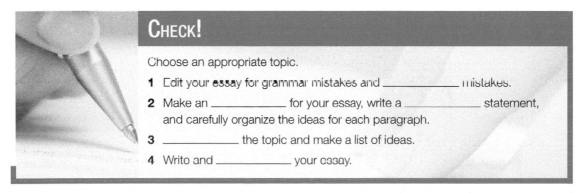

CHECK!

Choose an appropriate topic.

1 Edit your essay for grammar mistakes and _____ mistakes.

2 Make an _____ for your essay, write a _____ statement, and carefully organize the ideas for each paragraph.

3 _____ the topic and make a list of ideas.

4 Write and _____ your essay.

C. Practice

1   Read the essay topics. Write the letters from the missing sentences in the correct columns in the chart. There is one sentence that does not belong in the chart.

ESSAY TOPICS	FIRST DRAFT SENTENCES	FINAL DRAFT SENTENCES
The importance of saving money	Every body should have a savings account they are useful.	1 ___
Unnecessary luxuries	2 ___	For example, many experts agree that people do not need cable television.
Dangers of credit cards	3 ___	Although they may spend a great deal of money on certain luxuries, many people cannot afford these items.

a A lot of people can't afford stuff but they overspend with cards and they get in trouble.

b You don't really need a bunch of new clothing all the time.

c For example, lots of experts say peple don't need cable TV.

d Everyone should have a savings account because it is useful.

2   Read the essay excerpt and check (✓) the correct outline.

Many experts believe that the number of people who overspend has been increasing. They may overspend because they are depressed, they lack confidence, or they have a shopping addiction.

First, people who are depressed often feel better when they shop. However, this improved mood often does not last long. . . .

Second, some women who lack self-confidence may overspend on items such as new clothes. These things can help some women feel better about themselves. . . .

Third, some people overspend because they have an addiction. Shopping addicts cannot always control their behavior, and sometimes feel they need to shop in order to feel good. . . .

To conclude, there are many reasons why people may overspend. A feeling of depression or a lack of self-confidence may contribute to the problem. Some people have addictions they cannot control. No matter what the reason, people who overspend should seek help.

☐ **Outline A**
Introductory paragraph: With support, it is possible to stop overspending.
Body paragraph 1: friends can help by listening to problems
Body paragraph 2: interaction with family may improve confidence, which can help
Body paragraph 3: professional counselors can give advice
Conclusion: A strong support system can help people stop overspending.

☐ **Outline B**
Introductory paragraph: People may overspend because of depression, lack of confidence, or addiction.
Body paragraph 1: depressed people feel better when they shop
Body paragraph 2: some women who lack confidence buy clothes
Body paragraph 3: shopping addicts shop in order to feel good
Conclusion: People who overspend should seek help for their behavior.

D. Skill Quiz

Check (✓) the correct answer for each item.

1 When you choose an essay topic, think about what
   - ☐ a. your teacher is interested in.
   - ☐ b. you have already written about.
   - ☐ c. you are interested in and know about.

2 When you make a list of ideas,
   - ☐ a. use complete sentences.
   - ☐ b. use words and phrases.
   - ☐ c. add lots of details.

3 The purpose of an outline is to help writers
   - ☐ a. organize their thoughts and give the essay a logical flow.
   - ☐ b. choose an appropriate topic.
   - ☐ c. revise and edit their final draft.

4 The steps of prewriting are
   - ☐ a. choose an appropriate topic, revise the first draft, outline the essay.
   - ☐ b. choose an appropriate topic, make a list of ideas, outline the essay.
   - ☐ c. revise the first draft, edit the second draft, write a final draft.

5 When you revise the first draft of an essay, make sure that
   - ☐ a. it lists ideas using words and phrases.
   - ☐ b. all the words have more than four letters.
   - ☐ c. it has a logical flow and the ideas are clear.

6 When you edit an essay
   - ☐ a. look for spelling and grammar mistakes.
   - ☐ b. make a list of ideas.
   - ☐ c. create an outline.

7 Choose the correct essay-writing step shown in this text:
   Necessary Expenses
   • *rent*
   • *utilities*
   - ☐ a. outlining the essay
   - ☐ b. editing
   - ☐ c. making a list

8 Choose the correct essay-writing step shown in this text:
   Luxury Cars
   • *I want to learn more about luxury cars.*
   • *I think luxury cars are interesting.*
   - ☐ a. making a list
   - ☐ b. choosing a topic
   - ☐ c. outlining the essay

9 Choose the sentence that is most likely from the first draft of an essay.
   - ☐ a. For many years, people spend more and more money on luxury items many people paid for items with creddit cards
   - ☐ b. For many years, people spent a great deal of money on luxury items. Many people paid for these items with credit cards.
   - ☐ c. For many years, people spent increasing amounts of money on luxury items, and many people paid for them with credit cards.

10 Choose the best thesis statement for this essay topic: *The Science of Shopping Addiction.*
   - ☐ a. All addictions cause behavior that can harm the addict and others.
   - ☐ b. Shopping releases chemicals in the brain that make shopping addicts feel good.
   - ☐ c. A close circle of friends may help control compulsive shopping.

28

Analyzing an Essay

TECHNOLOGY IN SOCIETY

CONNECTING TO THE THEME

Do you think the writer effectively explains motion capture technology? Why or why not?

Computer programs that use motion capture (or "mocap") can help injured people. These programs record people's movements as they exercise. Exercisers put on a special suit and stand in front of a camera. Realistic virtual characters are created and move as the exercisers move. Mocap technology helps people correct mistakes because they can see these movements on the screen. The computer program can also check movements to make sure people do not hurt themselves. In conclusion, an exercise program with mocap technology is a useful tool for people with or without injuries.

A. Skill Presentation

After you write an essay, it is important to **analyze** it, or read it again carefully to see if you can make any improvements. Learning to analyze whether or not your essay contains certain key features will help you improve your writing. One of the first things you should do is **check that you have used the appropriate type of writing**. For example, if you wanted to describe how a place looks, you should have written a descriptive essay. If you wanted to show the similarities between two places, you should have written a comparison essay.

Next, you should **make sure your essay has a clear thesis statement**. Your thesis statement should state the main idea of the essay and include the main points that you write about in your body paragraphs. Check that your thesis statement is in the introductory paragraph, usually as the last sentence. Each aspect of the thesis statement will be described in its own body paragraph.

Check for unity when you analyze your essays. All of the information in the essay should relate to the thesis statement. Read each body paragraph in your essay, and make sure it has a clear topic sentence as well as supporting sentences that directly relate to the thesis statement.

Make sure your essay has a strong concluding paragraph. Read your concluding paragraph and make sure it restates the thesis statement, summarizes the most important points of the essay, and offers a suggestion, an opinion, or a prediction.

Finally, **make sure your essay has clear organization**. As you read your essay, make sure that your ideas are easy to follow. Remember that common ways to organize essays are time order (the order events happen), spatial order (the physical location of items), and point-by-point organization (writing about one aspect of the thesis statement in each body paragraph).

110

B. Over to You

1 Read the thesis statement from an essay about how mocap was used in a movie. Check (✓) three topic sentences from the body paragraphs. Remember to make sure they are directly related to the thesis statement.

Thesis Statement: Many critics agree that mocap made the characters appear realistic, believable, and interesting.

☐ a. Mocap gave the characters emotional expressions that brought their personalities to life.

☐ b. The movie made more money in ticket sales than any other movie in history.

☐ c. The characters moved like real people because of mocap technology.

☐ d. Mocap allowed the characters to interact realistically, making the story more interesting.

2 Read the introductory paragraph from an essay about mocap, and circle the correct answer for each item.

The History of Motion Capture Technology

The use of motion capture technology for animation started in the 1970s. It has changed and improved significantly over the years. Artists used to film people and then trace their movements. This helped them create realistic characters. Today, actors are filmed, and their movements are sent to a computer. Then, artists can change the images to create digital characters. Several important inventions in the last four decades have made motion capture an effective way to animate movies.

1 This paragraph is from *a descriptive | a comparison | an informal* essay about the history of mocap technology.

2 The thesis statement is the *last | first | second* sentence in the introductory paragraph.

3 The three body paragraphs will probably describe *some things that were invented since the 1970s | tools artists used before the 1970s to draw characters | several characters from different animated movies.*

4 The writer will probably organize this essay *in the order inventions were made | by the location of the parts of the inventions | in alphabetical order according to the artists' last names.*

CHECK!

1 Did you use the _____ type of writing?

2 Did you include a clear _____ statement that states the main idea of the essay?

3 Does your essay have _____? Is all the information directly _____ to the thesis statement?

4 Does your essay have a strong _____ paragraph that restates the thesis statement and _____ the most important points?

5 Does your essay have clear _____? Does it use _____ order, spatial order, or point-by-point organization?

C. Practice

1 **Read the thesis statement and the possible sentences from the body paragraphs. Check (✓) one sentence for each that does not relate to the thesis statement.**

Thesis Statement: Although there are many similarities between how mocap is used to make movies and to make video games, there are important differences.

1 Sentences from body paragraph 1:

☐ a. One difference between using mocap for movies and for video games is the way characters interact with viewers.

☐ b. In video games, on the other hand, the viewer controls one of the character's movements.

☐ c. Designers are paid a lot of money to create animation.

2 Sentences from body paragraph 2:

☐ a. Another difference is the environments that characters "live" in.

☐ b. Scenes in older TV programs often showed only one side of a room.

☐ c. Unlike movies, video game backgrounds allow the viewer to see in every direction.

3 Sentences from body paragraph 3:

☐ a. The Academy of Motion Picture Arts and Sciences now recognizes the importance of animated movies.

☐ b. A third difference between animation for movies and for video games is the use of sound.

☐ c. Characters in these movies speak to each other more often than they do in video games.

2 **Read the thesis statement and the three possible concluding paragraphs for the essay. Answer the questions.**

Thesis Statement: Programs that use mocap to train pilots are effective because they give pilots confidence, reduce risk, and help prepare pilots for different weather.

A In summary, pilots have a variety of skills. They must have good hand-eye coordination, be able to concentrate for long periods of time, and be in good physical shape. Without these special skills, a pilot will not be very successful.

B Mocap training programs help pilots gain confidence, provide practice without risk, and allow pilots to gain experience with different kinds of weather. These training programs are extremely useful, and more airlines will likely use them in the future. As technology improves, the programs will become more realistic, too.

C Because mocap training programs are so effective, more flight schools should use them. They are clearly useful for improving confidence. In addition, they allow pilots to practice safely and give pilots practice flying in different kinds of weather. Airlines should continue to use mocap training for both inexperienced pilots and experienced pilots.

___ **1** Which concluding paragraph does not relate to the essay?

___ **2** Which concluding paragraph offers a suggestion?

___ **3** Which concluding paragraph makes a prediction?

D. Skill Quiz

Check (✓) the correct answer for each item.

1 A thesis statement is found in
   - ☐ a. one of the body paragraphs.
   - ☐ b. the introductory paragraph.
   - ☐ c. the concluding paragraph.

2 What does a good thesis statement do?
   - ☐ a. It gives background information.
   - ☐ b. It states the main idea of the essay.
   - ☐ c. It summarizes the most important points from the essay.

3 What helps give an essay unity?
   - ☐ a. sentences that relate directly to the thesis statement
   - ☐ b. body paragraphs that discuss a variety of topics
   - ☐ c. a good balance of persuasion and cause–effect writing

4 An effective way to organize an essay is
   - ☐ a. by word length.
   - ☐ b. in the order events happen.
   - ☐ c. alphabetically.

5 Choose the type of essay that is most appropriate for an essay with this thesis statement: *The two movies both used motion capture technology, but they were extremely different.*
   - ☐ a. a descriptive essay
   - ☐ b. a cause–effect essay
   - ☐ c. a comparison essay

6 Choose the sentence from a body paragraph that is directly related to this thesis statement: *Motion capture is a useful tool to train firefighters.*
   - ☐ a. The technology simulates real fires but without real danger.
   - ☐ b. Some firefighters are paid to do their job, but others volunteer.
   - ☐ c. Well-trained firefighters save thousands of people every year.

7 Choose the sentence from a body paragraph that is directly related to this thesis statement: *Animated characters have many things in common with puppets.*
   - ☐ a. *Pinocchio* is about a puppet who wants to become a real boy.
   - ☐ b. The technology for animation is not used to create puppets.
   - ☐ c. Both puppets and animation require a person to control characters' movements.

8 Choose the correct sentence from a concluding paragraph in an essay with this thesis statement: *Walt Disney's work influenced motion capture technology.*
   - ☐ a. In conclusion, Walt Disney had many ideas that are used in motion capture technology today.
   - ☐ b. In summary, Tim Burton also influenced motion capture technology in many ways.
   - ☐ c. To conclude, fairy tales are still popular with children.

9 *To conclude, more people will use motion capture exercise programs in the future.* This sentence from a concluding paragraph
   - ☐ a. summarizes important points.
   - ☐ b. offers a suggestion.
   - ☐ c. makes a prediction.

10 Choose the best way a writer could organize an essay with this thesis statement: *Pixar has changed its technology significantly from the 1980s to today.*
   - ☐ a. List points alphabetically.
   - ☐ b. Put events in time order.
   - ☐ c. Describe things in the order of their physical location.

Review of Paragraph Types (Skills 15–18; 20)

This model of a **descriptive paragraph** describes a test kitchen at a university. The writer included **adjectives** and other details to describe exactly how the test kitchen looks.

> The Scientific Test Kitchen is a place where professors and students learn about new foods. In the front of the room, there are **five small** cooking areas. Each one contains a **gas** stove, a **large** sink, **wooden** cupboards, and a **huge** freezer. Next to the freezer are **three** microwaves. At the back of the room, there is a **private** meeting area. It contains a computer, a **flat-screen** TV, and **several folding** chairs. The equipment at the Scientific Test Kitchen allows people to learn about new experimental foods.

This paragraph uses spatial organization. It describes the kitchen from front to back.

This model of a **comparison paragraph** compares genetically modified salmon and wild salmon. Notice the words that are used to show how genetically modified salmon and wild salmon are **different**.

> There are several features that make genetically modified salmon and wild salmon different. **One difference is that** they grow in different environments. Wild salmon grow in rivers, **but** genetically modified salmon grow in small pools. **Another difference is** their diets. Wild salmon eat other wild fish. **In contrast**, genetically modified fish eat special food prepared by humans. **The most drastic difference is** how fast they grow. **Unlike** wild salmon, genetically modified salmon can grow in any temperature. For this reason, they grow all year, **whereas** wild salmon only grow six months during the year. It is clear that there are key differences between these two types of fish.

This paragraph uses point-by-point organization. Look at the sentences that introduce each point.

This model of a **cause–effect paragraph** gives the reasons why genetically modified rice may be dangerous. Notice the words that are used to show the **reasons** genetically modified rice may be dangerous.

> Some scientists argue that golden rice, which has been genetically modified to contain carotenoids, may be dangerous for two reasons. **One reason is** that some people may be allergic to it. Instead of making them healthier, it could make them very sick. **Another reason** golden rice may be dangerous is because it has not been tested enough. **Due to the fact that** scientists do not yet know the long-term effects of golden rice on health, there are some risks. Without further research, there are reasons to believe that golden rice may be harmful to human health.

This paragraph uses point-by-point organization. Notice the sentences that introduce each point.

This model of a **persuasive paragraph** gives the opinion that more golden rice should be grown for people living in poverty. The **supporting sentences** provide facts and examples to support this opinion.

> [O]More golden rice should be grown for people living in poverty. [SS]Golden rice can help prevent certain health problems, like blindness and other serious illnesses. [SS]The rice contains carotenoids, which can help people fight illnesses and stay healthy. [SS]Carotenoids are naturally found in many fruits and vegetables. [SS]However, people living in poorer areas cannot always afford to buy fruits and vegetables. [SS]Providing golden rice to people in these areas is the best way to improve their health. [CS]In conclusion, more farmers should produce golden rice to help people around the world.

The concluding sentence gives a suggestion about an action farmers should take.

Introduction to Essays (Skill 21)

The **introductory paragraph** introduces the topic of *vegetable oil fuel*. It gives interesting background information about the topic. The **thesis statement** clearly states the overall purpose of the essay – to discuss the advantages of using vegetable oil instead of gasoline. The rest of the essay will talk about specific advantages of vegetable oil fuel.

The **topic sentences** from the three **body paragraphs** of the essay tell what each paragraph will be about. They all relate to the thesis statement about advantages of vegetable oil fuel. These paragraphs support the thesis statement by providing specific examples of the advantages of using vegetable oil fuel.

In the **concluding paragraph**, the writer makes a prediction based on the information in the essay.

Fuel for the Future

These days, people are concerned about the environment. Many people want cars with engines that use alternative sources of fuel. Oil from plants, or vegetable oil, is one fuel source that people are talking about. ^{THS}There are many advantages to using vegetable oil instead of gasoline to power cars.

^{TS}First, vegetable oil fuel is much safer for the environment than gasoline. Vegetable oil does not release dangerous substances into the air. Gasoline does. Many people argue that this makes vegetable oil a better choice.

^{TS}Second, vegetable oil comes from plants, such as corn and soybeans. Plants are renewable, meaning farmers can grow them over and over again. Gasoline is not renewable. This makes vegetable oil a better long-term solution for our energy needs.

^{TS}Third, many people save money by switching to vegetable oil fuel. This renewable source of fuel is a much cheaper alternative than gasoline.

Since many people are concerned about the environment, it is important that they are aware of these possibilities. If we encourage the use of vegetable oil, we can help the environment and have plenty of energy to power our cars for years to come.

Descriptive Essays (Skill 25)

A Volcano Stops Travel

The introductory paragraph gives a basic description of a specific volcano and includes some general background information. The **thesis statement** shows that the essay will describe how the volcano's eruption was devastating to travel.

The 2010 eruption of the volcano "E15" affected almost every country in Europe. Ice and ash from the volcano caused major problems. Ice melted and flowed down the volcano, causing rivers to rise. The ash, however, caused the most problems. It filled the air and made it hard to see. As a result, airports in many European countries closed for more than a week. ᵀᴴˢThe eruption of E15 was devastating to travel throughout Europe.

Read the three **body paragraphs.** Each one has a **topic sentence** that relates to the main idea in the thesis statement, and tells what aspect of the essay topic will be described.

This essay organizes events by time. It describes the effects of the ash in the order they happened. The first body paragraph describes the first problem that happened because of the ash soon after the volcano erupted. The second body paragraph describes more problems that happened a few days later after wind blew the ash. The third body paragraph describes the airports after they had been closed a week later. Together, the three body paragraphs give a complete picture of how the eruption of this volcano hurt travel over time.

ᵀˢAsh from the volcano started causing problems after the eruption on April 14, 2010. The volcano blew huge amounts of gray ash into the sky. The ash was a thick, gray smoke, making it very difficult for airplane pilots to see. In addition, pilots feared that the ash would damage the engines of their airplanes. Flights into Iceland were canceled.

ᵀˢA few days after April 14, strong winds blew ash from E15 to several countries in Europe. This caused more problems. Airports in England, Finland, Sweden, and many other countries had to cancel flights, too. The airports became crowded, chaotic, and noisy. People on cell phones frantically made calls to make other arrangements.

ᵀˢA week later, many airports were still closed, but they became much quieter. There were no flights in or out of airports in many European countries. Word of the disaster spread, and the airports were calmer and less crowded as more people avoided them.

The concluding paragraph summarizes the main points of the essay by reminding the reader of the most important details and descriptions. It leaves the reader with an overall impression of the problems the volcano caused for travelers.

In conclusion, the eruption of E15 affected travelers around the world. Enormous clouds of ash from the volcano first caused problems with flights in Iceland. As the wind got stronger, it blew ash to other countries. Airports in other European countries had to cancel flights, as well. The airports buzzed with activity for several days because desperate travelers had no place to go. As the news of the catastrophe spread, airports slowly became less chaotic. Although the 2010 eruption E15 was disruptive, it was certainly memorable to many people.

Comparison Essays (Skill 26)

Mexican and Tex-Mex Foods

The **introductory paragraph** gives background information about how foods from other countries are adapted for Americans' tastes. The **thesis statement** tells the reader that the essay will explain how Mexican food and Tex-Mex food are different.

> There are many different cultures in the United States. As a result, there are many different types of foods. Many of these foods are adapted for Americans' tastes. For instance, Tex-Mex food, which was adapted from Mexican food, is extremely popular in the United States. Some of this food is similar to food in Mexico, but not all of it is the same. [THS]There are some important differences between Mexican and Tex-Mex foods.

Look at the excerpt of the three **body paragraphs**. Each **topic sentence** relates directly to the topic in the thesis statement, and tells what aspect of the main idea will be compared in that paragraph. The first body paragraph compares the way Mexican and Tex-Mex foods are served. The second body paragraph compares the ingredients used in Mexican and Tex-Mex foods. The third paragraph shows that sometimes the two types of food are completely different.

> [TS]One difference is that some Mexican and Tex-Mex foods are served in different ways. Tex-Mex restaurants in the United States usually serve chips and salsa before dinner. Although salsa is popular in Mexico, people do not typically eat it with chips before dinner.
>
> [TS]Another difference between Tex-Mex and Mexican foods is that the ingredients are not always the same. Tex-Mex food often uses ground beef, whereas Mexican food often uses chicken. In addition, Tex-Mex food is often made with yellow or orange cheese, but Mexican food is usually made with soft white cheese.
>
> [TS]Finally, some Mexican and Tex-Mex foods are completely different. A *sope* is a dish with meat, vegetables, and cheese. It is on many menus in Mexico. However, many Tex-Mex restaurants do not serve them. *Sopapillas* are a common Tex-Mex dessert, but they are not a traditional Mexican food.

The first sentence in the **concluding paragraph** restates the main idea of the essay. The second and third sentences summarize the main points of the essay. The last sentence offers an opinion.

> In conclusion, there are many clear differences between Mexican and Tex-Mex food. The way meals are served, the ingredients, and the actual dishes can be completely different. Both kinds of food appeal to many people in the United States. Everyone should understand the differences between Mexican and Tex-Mex foods.

academic writing: writing for school; it usually includes more formal language than other kinds of writing (e.g., personal communication) (See Skill 12.)

action verb: a verb such as *eat*, *celebrate*, or *give* that describes an action; it tells what a noun is doing

analyze: to look at something in a systematic and careful way (See Skill 28.)

audience: the people who will read your writing, for example, a teacher or classmates (See Skill 9.)

auxiliary verb: a verb such as *do* or *be* that is used before a main verb in a sentence (See Skill 6.)

body paragraph: a paragraph in an essay that gives specific information about points from the thesis statement; it comes after the introductory paragraph and before the concluding paragraph (See Skill 23.)

cause–effect paragraph: a paragraph that can explain the reasons why an event or situation happens or give the results of an event or situation (See Skill 17.)

citation: detailed information about an outside source of information used in a piece of writing; citations are necessary for quotations and paraphrases (See Skill 19.)

clarity: the quality of being clear and easy to understand; the use of specific adjectives, action verbs, and the appropriate use of nouns and pronouns help create clarity in a piece of writing (See Skill 10.)

clause: a group of words that has a subject and a verb

coherence: the clear organization of sentences in a piece of writing; putting sentences in logical order and using transition words and phrases are ways to create coherence (See Skill 13.)

comma: a punctuation mark (,) used, for example, to separate certain clauses in a sentence or to separate three or more items in a list

comma splice: two or more independent clauses connected only by a comma (See Skill 7.)

comparison essay: an essay that compares two or more things; it shows how they are alike or how they are different (See Skill 26.)

comparison paragraph: a paragraph that compares two or more things or ideas; it shows how they are alike or how they are different (See Skill 16.)

complex sentence: a sentence with an independent clause and a dependent clause joined by a subordinating conjunction, such as *after*, *because*, *if*, or *when* (See Skill 1.)

compound sentence: a sentence with two independent clauses joined by a comma and a coordinating conjunction such as *and*, *or*, *but*, or *so* (See Skill 1.)

concluding paragraph: a paragraph that restates the main idea in an essay and summarizes the main points from the body paragraphs. It can also give a prediction, a suggestion, or an opinion; it is the last paragraph in an essay (See Skill 24.)

concluding sentence: a sentence that can restate the main idea in a paragraph, offer a suggestion, or make a prediction about the topic; it is often the last sentence in a paragraph (See Skill 5.)

conjunction: a word such as *and*, *or*, *when*, or *because* that connects single words, phrases, or clauses

contraction: a shortened form of a word or combination of words; it uses an apostrophe

controlling idea: an idea that tells what kind of information will be given about the topic in a paragraph; it is expressed in the topic sentence (See Skill 3.)

coordinating conjunction: a word such as *and*, *or*, *but*, or *so* that joins two independent clauses in a compound sentence (See Skill 1.)

dependent clause: a group of words that has a subject and verb but does not express a complete idea; it cannot be used alone as a complete sentence (See Skill 1.)

descriptive essay: an essay that gives a detailed picture of a topic; it describes how something looks, feels, smells, tastes, or sounds (See Skill 25.)

descriptive paragraph: a paragraph that gives a detailed picture of a topic; it describes how something looks, feels, smells, tastes, or sounds (See Skill 15.)

detail: a specific fact or piece of information

edit: to correct grammar, spelling, and punctuation mistakes in a piece of writing (See Skill 27.)

essay: a piece of writing with several paragraphs about one topic (See Skill 21.)

fact: something that is true and can be proven

final draft: a piece of writing that is considered finished; it is usually not considered final until there has been a first draft, revising, and editing (See Skill 27.)

first draft: an initial piece of writing that is done after prewriting but before the final draft (See Skill 27.)

first person: a point of view in writing that often includes pronouns such as *I* or *me*; it is used when people write about themselves (See Skill 12.)

five-paragraph essay: an essay format in which each paragraph has a special role; it includes an introductory paragraph, three body paragraphs, and a concluding paragraph (See Skill 21.)

formal: a style of writing used when it is not appropriate to show familiarity, such as in business; a college essay is an example of formal writing (See Skill 9.)

full form: the form of a word or group of words in which each letter appears; for example, *cannot* is the full form of the contraction *can't*

hook: a sentence that gets the reader's attention; it is usually the first sentence in the introductory paragraph of an essay (See Skill 22.)

independent clause: a group of words that has a subject and a verb and expresses a complete idea; it can be used alone as a complete sentence (See Skill 1.)

informal: a style of writing used with friends and family often based on personal experiences; personal e-mails or personal blogs are examples of informal writing (See Skill 12.)

introductory paragraph: a paragraph that gets the reader's attention and gives general information about the topic of an essay; it is the first paragraph in an essay (See Skill 22.)

irrelevant sentence: a sentence that does not relate to the main idea of a paragraph (See Skill 2.)

list: words or phrases that are arranged one below the other (See Skill 27.)

lowercase letter: the small form of a letter

main idea: what a piece of writing is about

main verb: a verb used alone, or with an auxiliary verb, in a sentence

noun: a word for a person, place, thing, or idea

noun phrase: a group of words that functions as a noun in a sentence

opinion: a belief that cannot be proven (See Skill 12.)

order of importance: a way of organizing ideas according to how important they are; for example, ordering ideas from most to least important or from least to most important (See Skill 9.)

organization: the arrangement of things in a special order

outline: a detailed list that helps writers organize their ideas and make sure their writing has a logical flow (See Skill 27.)

paragraph: a group of sentences about one topic; the sentences have a special format (See Skill 2.)

parallel structure: the use of similar word patterns in lists; for example, listing present tense verbs with other present tense verbs or listing prepositional phrases with other prepositional phrases (See Skill 8.)

paraphrase: to put another writer's idea in your own words (See Skill 19.)

persuasive paragraph: a paragraph in which the writer gives an opinion about a topic and tries to convince readers the opinion is correct; it can also try to convince readers to take action (See Skill 18.)

phrase: a group of words that forms part of a sentence

plagiarism: the use of another person's ideas or information without providing an appropriate citation. At colleges and universities in North America, plagiarism is a very serious offense; it is considered stealing (See Skill 19.)

point-by-point organization: a way of organizing a piece of writing in which points about different things or ideas are presented, one at a time (See Skill 16.)

preposition: a word such as *in*, *on*, or *at* that helps show location or time

prepositional phrase: a preposition followed by a noun; for example, *at noon*, *in Boston*, or *on computers*

prewriting: the first steps taken when you write an essay; these can include choosing an appropriate topic, making a list of ideas, and creating an outline (See Skill 27.)

pronoun: a word that is used in place of a noun

punctuation: special marks that are used to show the divisions between phrases and sentences

purpose: the reason you are writing; for example, to inform readers about something new or to persuade readers what to do or what to think (See Skill 9.)

quotation: another writer's exact words (See Skill 19.)

quotation marks: punctuation marks (") used before and after a quotation to show that the words are someone else's (See Skill 19.)

relevant sentence: a sentence that relates to the main idea of a paragraph (See Skill 2.)

revise: to fix the overall problems with the structure of a piece of writing (See Skill 27.)

run-on sentence: two or more independent clauses connected without a comma or a conjunction (See Skill 7.)

second person: a point of view in writing that often includes the pronoun *you*; it is used when people write to someone else (See Skill 12.)

sentence: a group of words that has a subject and a verb and expresses a complete idea

sentence fragment: a group of words that does not express a complete idea; a sentence fragment may be missing a subject or a verb, or it may be a dependent clause by itself (See Skill 6.)

simple sentence: a sentence with only one independent clause; it expresses only one complete idea (See Skill 1.)

source: someone or something from which a writer gets information (See Skill 19.)

spatial organization: a way of organizing a piece of writing according to where things are located; for example, describing something from bottom to top or from front to back (See Skill 15.)

specific adjective: an adjective such as *acceptable*, *dangerous*, or *skilled* that gives vivid or precise details about a noun (See Skill 10.)

subject: the person, place, thing, or idea that does the action in a sentence

subject–verb agreement: agreement in number between a subject and verb; a singular subject is matched with a singular verb, and a plural subject is matched with a plural verb

subordinating conjunction: a conjunction such as *after*, *because*, *if*, or *when* that joins a dependent clause to an independent clause in a complex sentence (See Skill 1.)

summarize: to briefly state the most important information in a piece of writing

supporting sentence: a sentence that gives facts, examples, or details to support the main idea in a paragraph (See Skill 4.)

synonym: a word or phrase that has the same or nearly the same meaning as another word or phrase (See Skill 13.)

thesis statement: a sentence that states the main idea of an essay; it is usually at the end of an introductory paragraph (See Skill 21.)

third person: a point of view in writing that often includes pronouns such as *he* or *they*; it is used when people write about other people (See Skill 12.)

time order (also called chronological order): the order in which events happen in time (See Skill 13.)

topic: who or what a piece of writing is about (See Skill 3.)

topic sentence: a sentence that expresses the main idea of a paragraph; it is often the first sentence in a paragraph (See Skill 3.)

transition phrases: phrases such as *for example*, *on the other hand*, or *in conclusion* that connect sentences in a paragraph; they help organize the ideas in a paragraph (See Skill 2.)

transition words: words such as *first*, *then*, or *finally* that connect sentences in a paragraph; they help organize the ideas in a paragraph (See Skill 2.)

unity: when all the information in a paragraph or an essay relates directly to the main idea (See Skill 11.)

verb: a word that describes an action or a state; it tells what the subject in a sentence is doing or being

What are the most common words in academic English? Which words appear most frequently in readings in different academic subject areas? Dr. Averil Coxhead, who is currently a Senior Lecturer at Victoria University of Wellington in New Zealand, did research to try to answer this question. The result was the **Academic Word List** (AWL), a list of 570 words or word families that appear in academic readings in many different academic fields. These words are extremely useful for students to know. In *Skills for Effective Writing*, you will encounter a number of these words in context.

The following is a list of the AWL words in *Skills for Effective Writing 3* and the Skills where they appear.

academic	9; 12; 19	beneficial	9
academy	12; 28	benefit	6; 11; 19–21; 25
access	5; 8; 22–24	briefly	24
accurately	22	capable	23; 25
achieve	3; 23	challenge	9–10; 23
achievement	17	challenging	15
adapt	14; 26	chart	1; 3–4; 6–8; 11–14; 16–18; 20–21; 23
adjust	11		
adult	8; 10; 13–14; 17–18; 25	chemical	27
affect	4; 8; 14; 25	citation	19
aid	12	clarity	9–10
alternative	6; 21	clause	1; 6–8
analyze	22; 28	coherence	9; 13
annually	12	coherent	9; 13
approach	24	colleague	23
appropriate	2; 5; 9–10; 12; 15; 17–18; 20; 22–23; 25–28	comment	2
		communicate	2; 18–19
appropriately	13; 24	communication	6; 8; 18–19
approximately	9	community	12; 24
area	18; 20; 25–26	complex	1; 6
aspect	16; 25–26; 28	compound	1
assignment	7	computer	5–6; 8; 13; 15–16; 18; 20–23; 28
assist	9	concentrate	7; 28
assistance	25	concentration	7
attitude	9	conclude	2; 5; 13; 18; 24–28
author	9; 16; 19	conclusion	2; 5; 10; 17–18; 20–21; 24–28
automated	16	conference	6
automatic	16	consequently	17; 20
automatically	5	consist	10; 22
available	5; 14; 16; 22; 26	constant	15
aware	21	consume	10
awareness	19	consumer	13

remove	27	text	8; 12; 16; 19; 23; 27
require	6; 12; 16; 19; 28	theory	17
research	4–5; 7; 10; 17; 19–20; 27	thesis	21–28
researcher	4; 15; 18–19; 23	topic	2–5; 11; 14–18; 20–28
resource	6; 11; 24	trace	28
respond	13	tradition	10
response	13	traditional	6; 14; 26
reveal	24	traditionally	9; 26
revise	10; 27	transfer	8
revolution	15	transition	2; 9; 13; 24
role	2; 4; 10; 17; 21	transportation	16
schedule	23	unique	22
secure	6	unmotivated	17
security	3; 22	utility	27
seek	11; 27	vary	1; 3; 14
select	10	violate	22
significant	4; 10	virtual	2; 28
significantly	4; 28	vision	4; 22
signify	10	volunteer	28
similar	4; 8–9; 13–14; 16; 18; 22; 26	whereas	16; 20; 26
similarity	4; 14; 16; 20; 28	widespread	19
similarly	4; 16; 20		
simulate	28		
site	2; 6; 23–24		
source	19; 21; 24		
specific	3–4; 9–13; 15; 17; 19–23; 25–26		
specifically	27		
strategy	13; 18		
stress	17		
structure	8		
style	26		
stylish	15		
summarize	2; 5; 13; 21; 24–26; 28		
summary	5, 9, 13; 17–18; 21; 24 26; 28		
survey	6; 11		
survive	25		
sustainability	6		
sustainable	6		
task	17; 23		
team	11; 23; 25		
technique	13; 18–19		
technology	2; 5–6; 8; 11; 19; 22–23; 28		
temporary	25		